CSK

CSK

CSK

CSK

CSK

McGRAW-HILL'S OUR NATION, OUR WORLD

MEETING PEOPLE

School, Self, Families, Neighborhood, and Our Country

GOING PLACES

People in Groups, Filling Needs in Communities and on Farms

COMMUNITIES

Geography and History of Cities in the United States, Canada, and Mexico

EARTH'S REGIONS

Geography and Ways of Living on Five Continents, Studying the 50 States

UNITED STATES

Chronological History of the United States, North America Today

THE WORLD

World History, Ancient Civilizations, Important Nations Today

CONSULTANTS

BONNIE AMASON
A.M. Davis Elementary School
Richmond, Virginia

DR. L. JO ANNE BUGGEY
Educational Consultant
Minneapolis, Minnesota

MILDRED CROWELL
Jamestown Academy
Williamsburg, Virginia

CORA DVERSDALL
Parkview Elementary School
Oklahoma City, Oklahoma

DON FELICE
Falling Creek Middle School
Richmond, Virginia

JUDY A. FISHER
Dennis Elementary School
Oklahoma City, Oklahoma

CAROLYN FITZGERALD
Powhatan Middle School
Powhatan, Virginia

SANDY HANNINGTON
Central Elementary School
Yukon, Oklahoma

CAROLYN HERBST
Eli Whitney Vocational High School
Brooklyn, New York

DR. RONALD J. HERMANSEN
Staff Assistant, Social Studies
Granite School District
Salt Lake City, Utah

DR. LEONORE HOFFMANN
City University of New York
Former Director, Federal Projects
Modern Language Association

SISTER M. JEANNETTE, I.H.M.
Archdiocese of Philadelphia
Philadelphia, Pennsylvania

ELAINE S. JONES
Woodinville, Washington

SISTER SHARON KERRIGAN
Diocese of Joliet
Joliet, Illinois

HERELYNN KIDD
Shedeck Elementary School
Yukon, Oklahoma

MARY S. McDADE
St. Joseph's School
Petersburg, Virginia

JEAN McGRADY
Western Oaks Elementary School
Bethany, Oklahoma

SISTER GLENN ANNE McPHEE
Archdiocese of Los Angeles
Los Angeles, California

ELAINE MAGNUSON
Canyon Creek Elementary School
Bothell, Washington

SHERRILL MILLER
Seattle, Washington

FRED PEFFER
Central Elementary School
Yukon, Oklahoma

SUZANNE PHELPS
Traub Elementary School
Midwest City, Oklahoma

BETSY PIERCE
Hamilton-Holmes Elementary School
King William, Virginia

SUSIE REYNOLDS
Overholser Elementary School
Bethany, Oklahoma

JOANNE ROBERTSON
Redmond, Washington

SISTER ANN SCHAFER
St. Luke's School
Seattle, Washington

KENNETH SUNDIN
Hollywood Hill Elementary School
Woodinville, Washington

JANE THOMAS
Robious Middle School
Midlothian, Virginia

NORA WASHINGTON
Byrd Primary School
Hadensville, Virginia

RONALD GRIGSBY KIRCHEM
Editorial Consultant and Contributing Writer

Editor in Chief: Leonard Martelli
Senior Editor: Alma Graham
Editing and Styling: Linda Richmond, Caroline Levine
Photo Editing Supervision: Rosemary O'Connell
Production Supervision: Salvador Gonzales, Judith Tisdale

Assistant Editors: James Allan Bartz, Ronald J. Bogus
Photo Editor: Alan Forman
Design by: Function Thru Form Inc.
Cover Design by: Blaise Zito Associates
Cover Photography by: Bill Holland

COMMUNITIES

BY Joyce Speas, Leonard Martelli,
Alma Graham, Lynn Cherryholmes

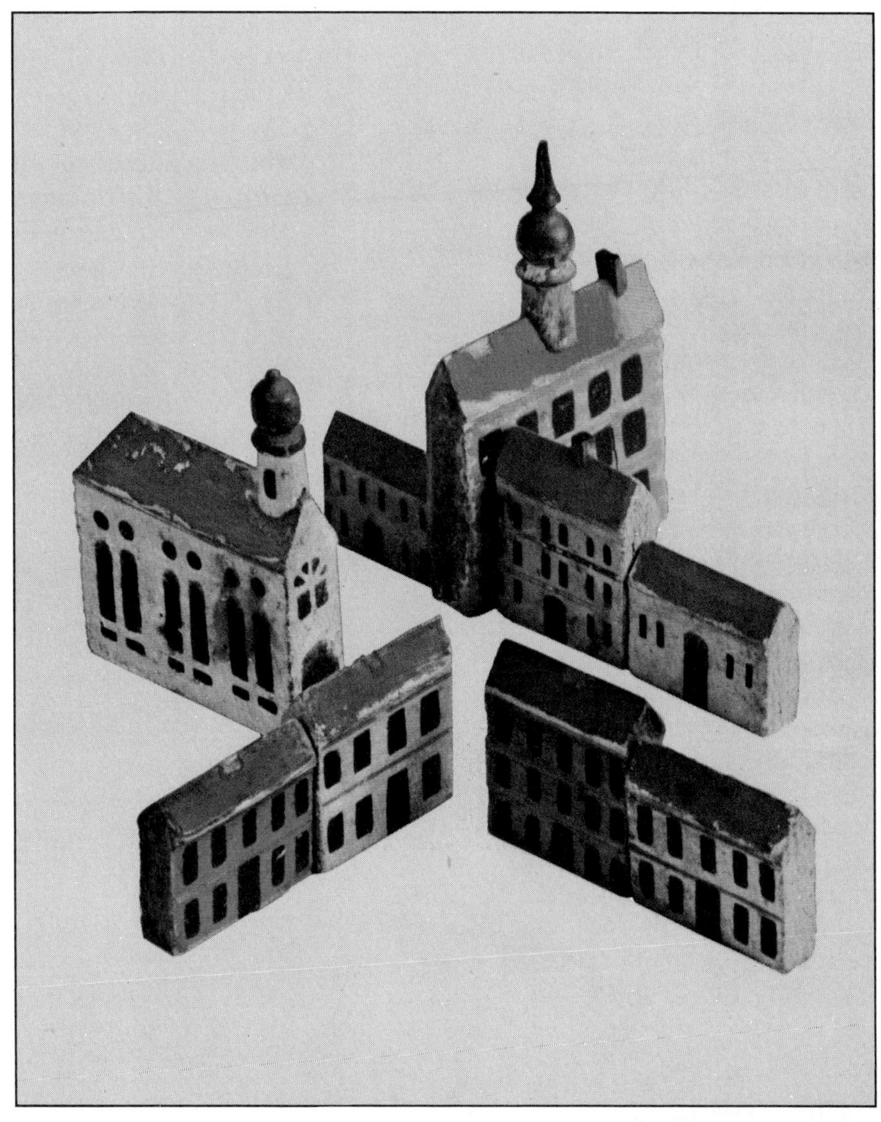

WEBSTER DIVISION, McGRAW-HILL BOOK COMPANY

New York St. Louis San Francisco Auckland Bogotá Düsseldorf
Johannesburg London Madrid Mexico Montreal New Delhi
Panama Paris São Paulo Singapore Sydney Tokyo Toronto

LIST OF MAPS AND CHARTS

FUN FACTS AND STRANGE FACTS

TIME LINES

WHERE WE ARE IN TIME AND PLACE

ISBN 0-07-039943-3

2 3 4 5 6 7 8 9 10 KP KP 91 90 89 88 87 86 85 84 83

CONTENTS

1777

1795

1818

1861

1912

1959

ATLAS

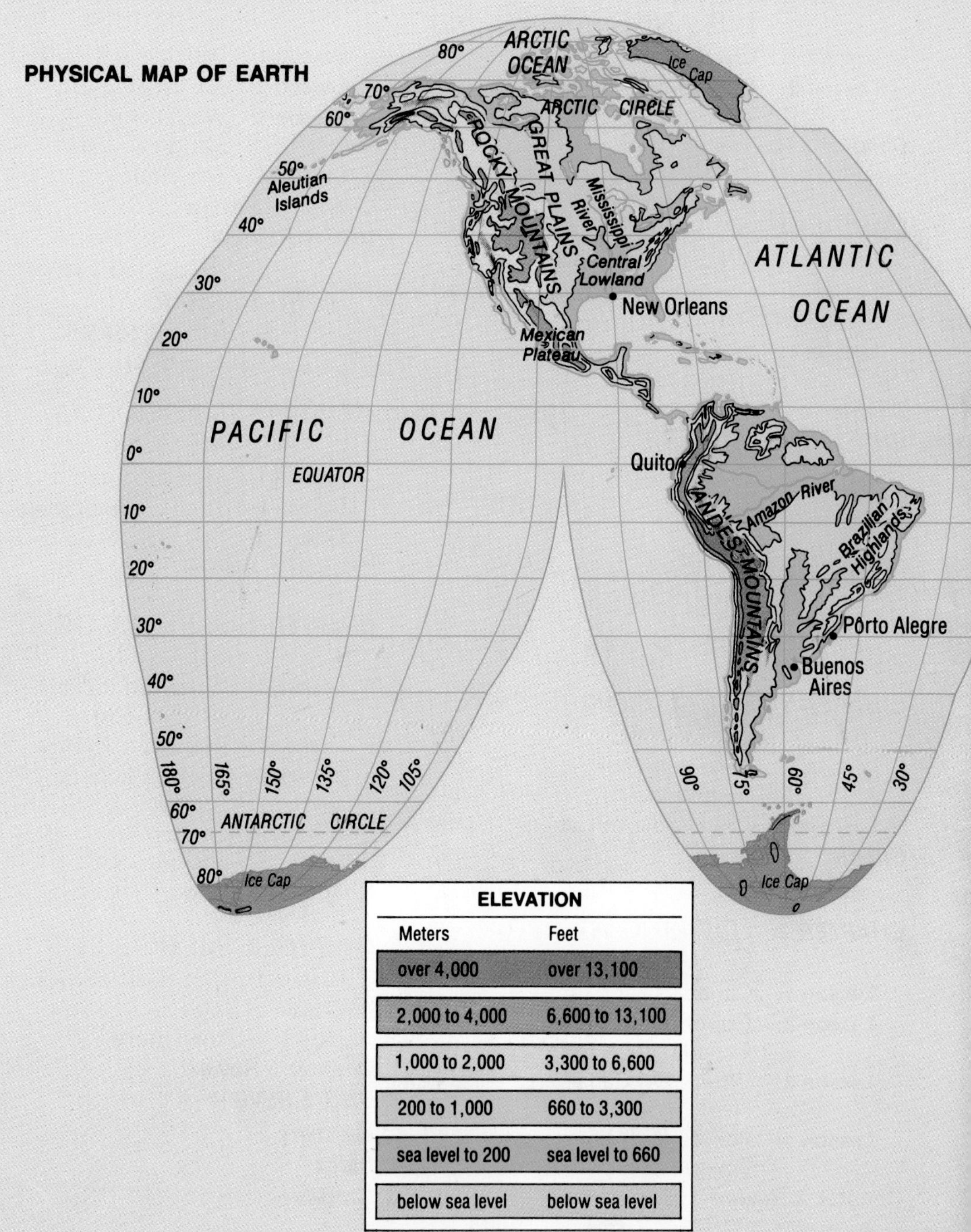

PHYSICAL MAP OF EARTH
ARCTIC OCEAN
Ice Cap
ARCTIC CIRCLE
80°
70°
60°
50°
Aleutian Islands
40°
30°
20°
10°
0°
ROCKY MOUNTAINS
GREAT PLAINS
Mississippi River
Central Lowland
New Orleans
Mexican Plateau
ATLANTIC OCEAN
PACIFIC OCEAN
EQUATOR
Quito
Amazon River
ANDES MOUNTAINS
Brazilian Highlands
Pôrto Alegre
Buenos Aires
180°
165°
150°
135°
120°
105°
90°
75°
60°
45°
30°
ANTARCTIC CIRCLE
Ice Cap
Ice Cap
ELEVATION
Meters
Feet
over 4,000
over 13,100
2,000 to 4,000
6,600 to 13,100
1,000 to 2,000
3,300 to 6,600
200 to 1,000
660 to 3,300
sea level to 200
sea level to 660
below sea level
below sea level

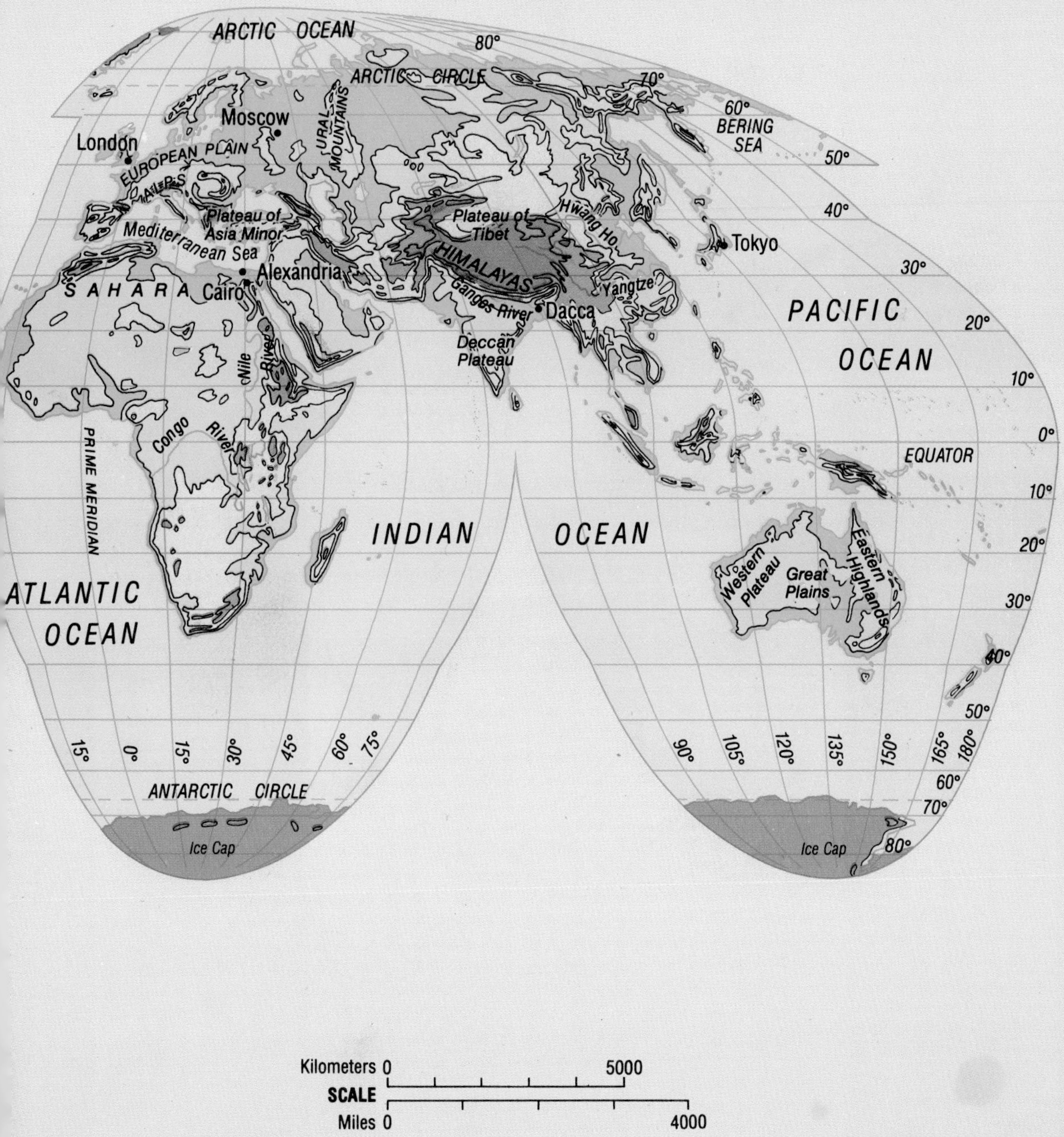

ARCTIC OCEAN
80°
ARCTIC CIRCLE
70°
60°
BERING SEA
50°
40°
30°
20°
10°
0°
10°
20°
30°
40°
50°
60°
70°
80°
London
Moscow
EUROPEAN PLAIN
URAL MOUNTAINS
ALPS
Plateau of Asia Minor
Mediterranean Sea
Alexandria
Cairo
SAHARA
Nile River
Congo River
Plateau of Tibet
HIMALAYAS
Hwang Ho
Tokyo
Yangtze
Ganges River
Dacca
Deccan Plateau
PACIFIC OCEAN
EQUATOR
PRIME MERIDIAN
ATLANTIC OCEAN
INDIAN OCEAN
Western Plateau
Great Plains
Eastern Highlands
15°
0°
15°
30°
45°
60°
75°
90°
105°
120°
135°
150°
165°
180°
ANTARCTIC CIRCLE
Ice Cap
Ice Cap
Kilometers 0
5000
SCALE
Miles 0
4000

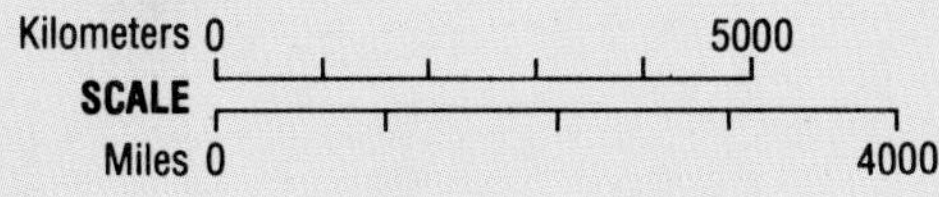

POLITICAL MAP OF EARTH

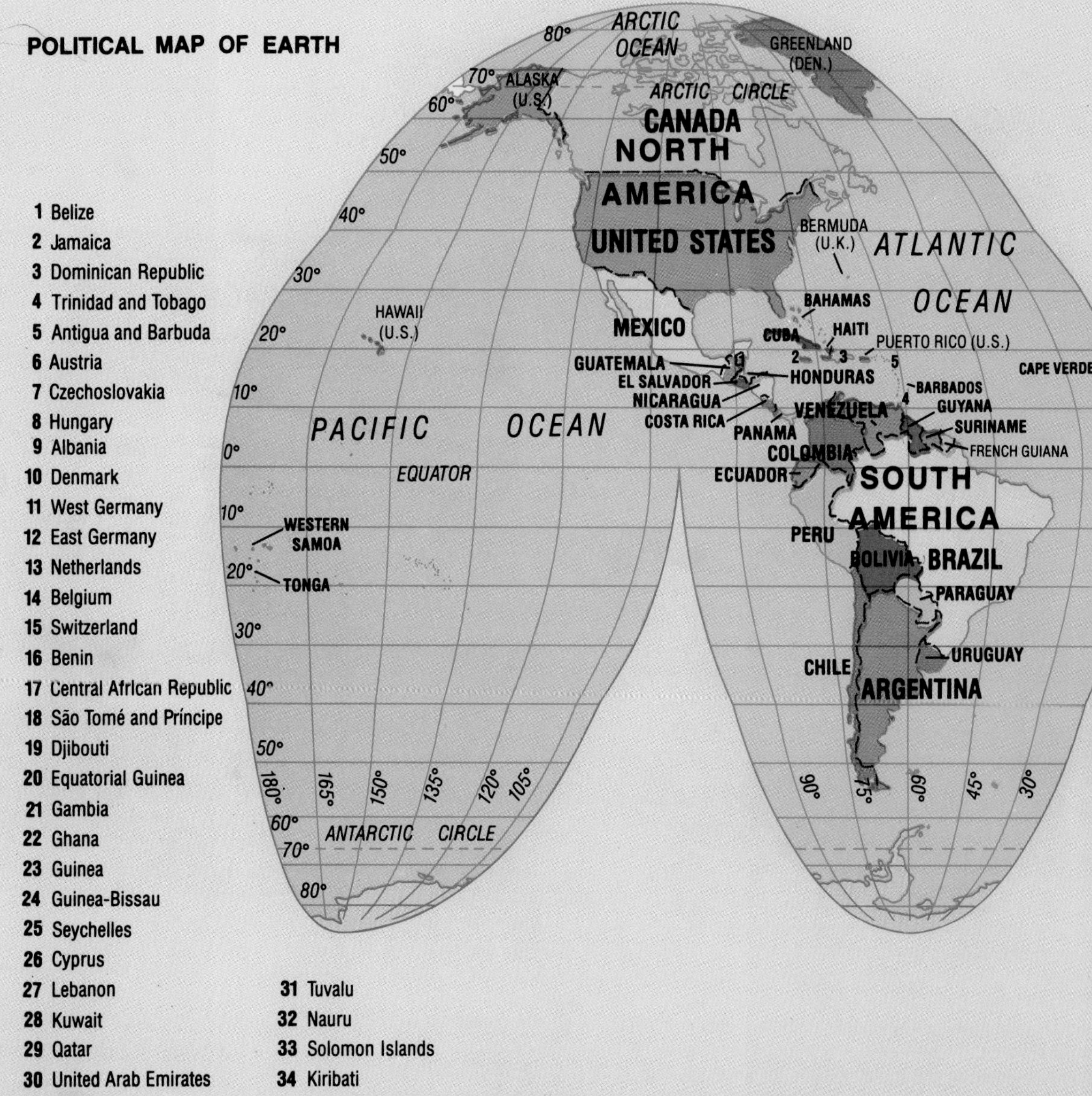

1 Belize
2 Jamaica
3 Dominican Republic
4 Trinidad and Tobago
5 Antigua and Barbuda
6 Austria
7 Czechoslovakia
8 Hungary
9 Albania
10 Denmark
11 West Germany
12 East Germany
13 Netherlands
14 Belgium
15 Switzerland
16 Benin
17 Central African Republic
18 São Tomé and Príncipe
19 Djibouti
20 Equatorial Guinea
21 Gambia
22 Ghana
23 Guinea
24 Guinea-Bissau
25 Seychelles
26 Cyprus
27 Lebanon
28 Kuwait
29 Qatar
30 United Arab Emirates
31 Tuvalu
32 Nauru
33 Solomon Islands
34 Kiribati

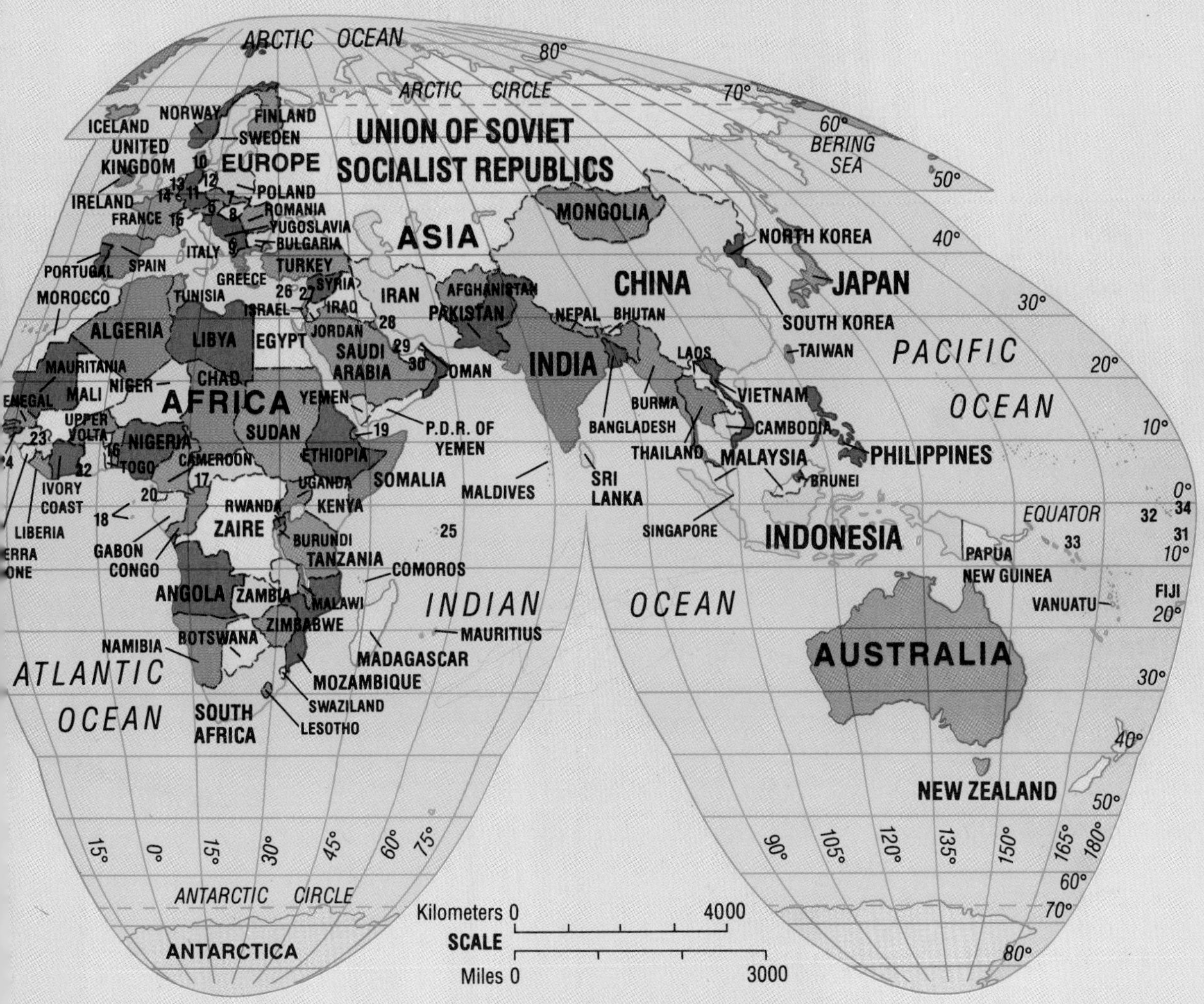
ARCTIC OCEAN
ARCTIC CIRCLE
UNION OF SOVIET SOCIALIST REPUBLICS
EUROPE
ASIA
CHINA
MONGOLIA
NORTH KOREA
JAPAN
SOUTH KOREA
TAIWAN
PACIFIC OCEAN
BERING SEA
ICELAND
NORWAY
FINLAND
SWEDEN
UNITED KINGDOM
IRELAND
FRANCE
POLAND
ROMANIA
YUGOSLAVIA
BULGARIA
ITALY
PORTUGAL
SPAIN
GREECE
TURKEY
SYRIA
ISRAEL
IRAQ
IRAN
JORDAN
AFGHANISTAN
PAKISTAN
NEPAL
BHUTAN
INDIA
BANGLADESH
BURMA
LAOS
VIETNAM
CAMBODIA
THAILAND
MALAYSIA
BRUNEI
PHILIPPINES
SINGAPORE
INDONESIA
PAPUA NEW GUINEA
SRI LANKA
MALDIVES
MOROCCO
TUNISIA
ALGERIA
LIBYA
EGYPT
SAUDI ARABIA
OMAN
YEMEN
P.D.R. OF YEMEN
MAURITANIA
MALI
NIGER
CHAD
AFRICA
SUDAN
ETHIOPIA
SOMALIA
UPPER VOLTA
NIGERIA
TOGO
CAMEROON
IVORY COAST
LIBERIA
GABON
CONGO
RWANDA
ZAIRE
UGANDA
KENYA
BURUNDI
TANZANIA
COMOROS
ANGOLA
ZAMBIA
MALAWI
ZIMBABWE
NAMIBIA
BOTSWANA
MOZAMBIQUE
SWAZILAND
LESOTHO
SOUTH AFRICA
MADAGASCAR
MAURITIUS
INDIAN OCEAN
ATLANTIC OCEAN
AUSTRALIA
NEW ZEALAND
VANUATU
FIJI
EQUATOR
ANTARCTIC CIRCLE
ANTARCTICA
Kilometers 0 4000
SCALE
Miles 0 3000

THE EASTERN UNITED STATES

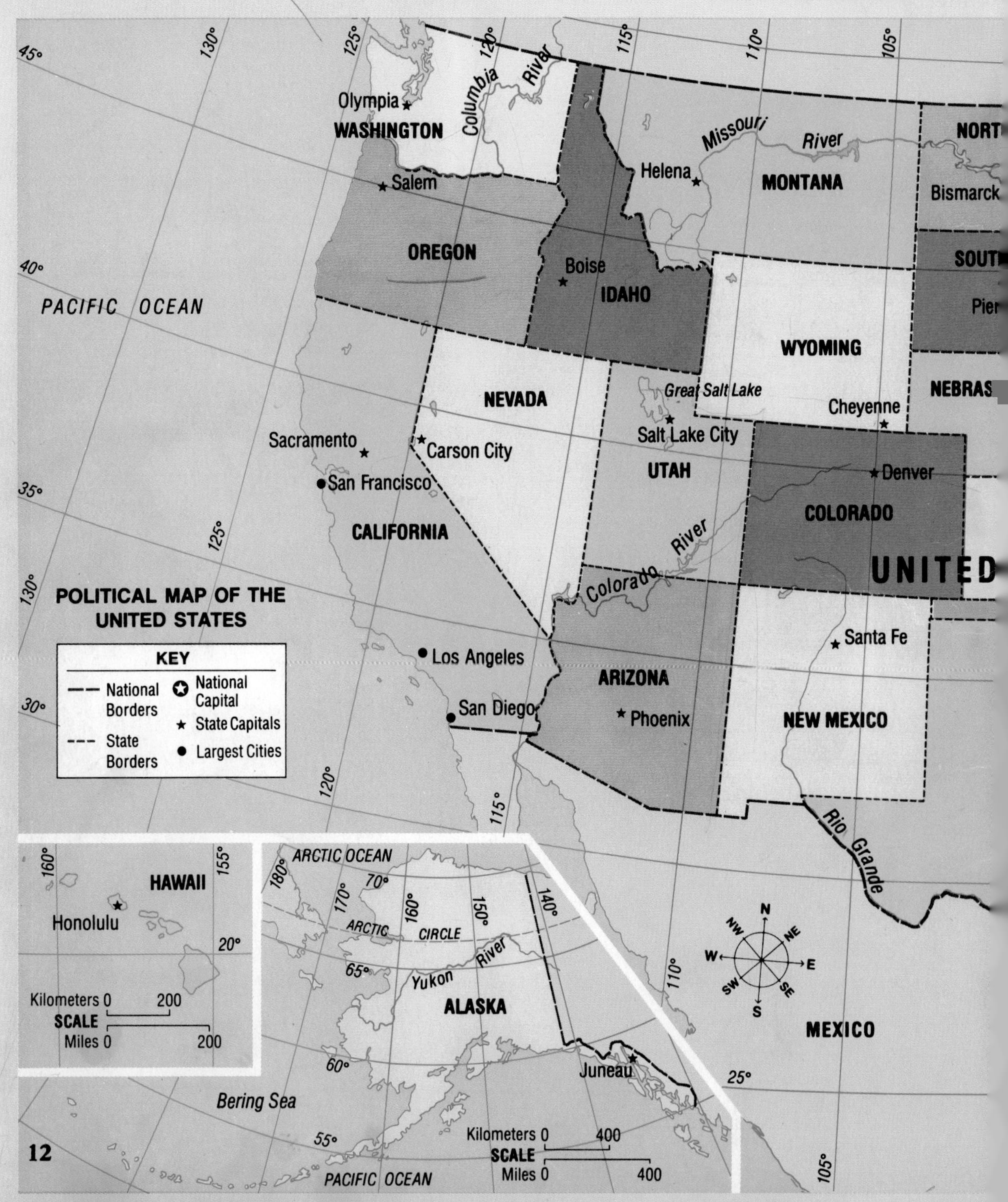

UNIT 1

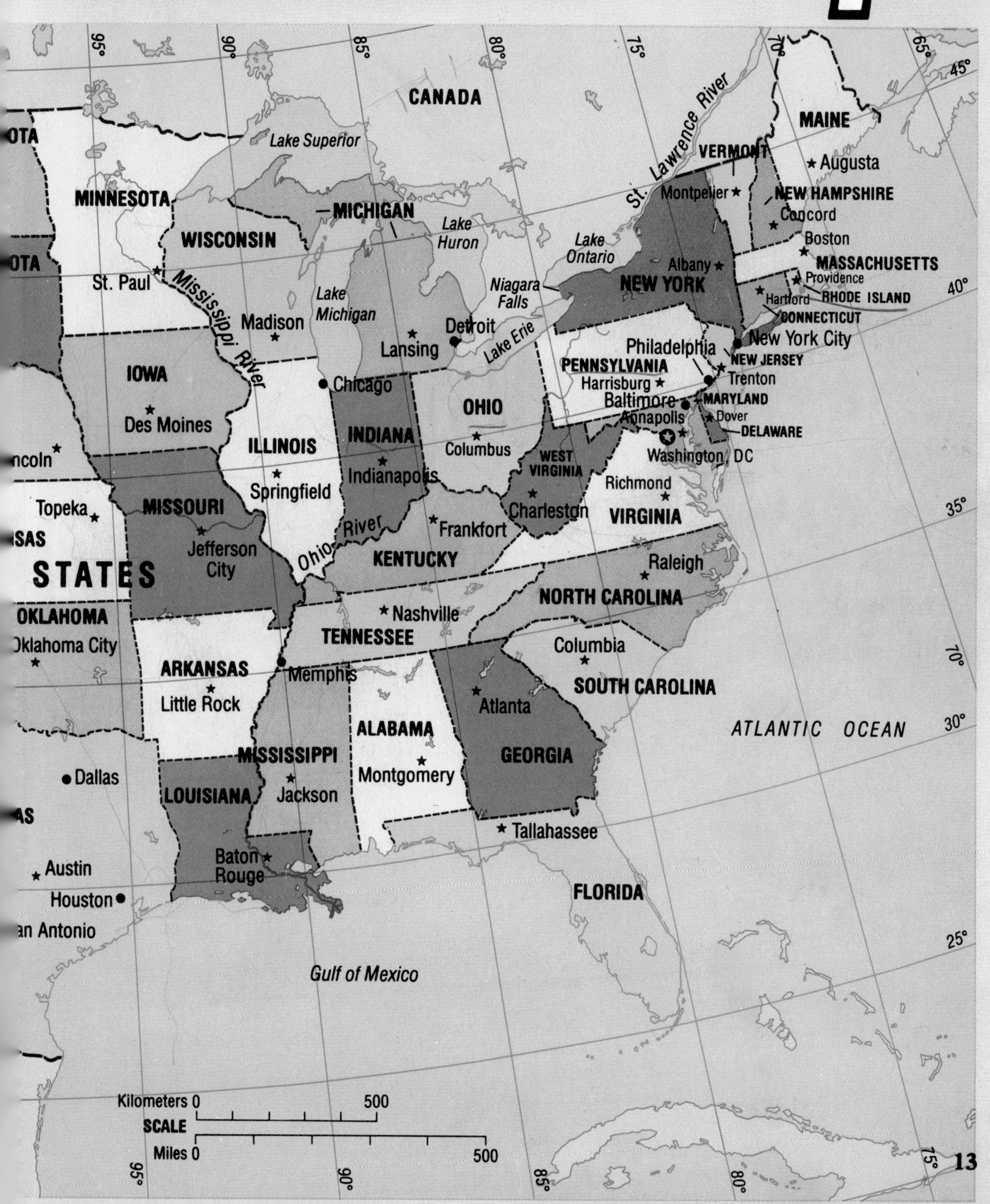
CANADA
Lake Superior
St. Lawrence River
MAINE
VERMONT
Augusta
MINNESOTA
MICHIGAN
Montpelier
NEW HAMPSHIRE
Concord
Lake Huron
WISCONSIN
Lake Ontario
Boston
MASSACHUSETTS
Albany
St. Paul
Mississippi River
Lake Michigan
Niagara Falls
NEW YORK
Providence
RHODE ISLAND
Hartford
CONNECTICUT
Madison
Detroit
Lansing
Lake Erie
Philadelphia
New York City
IOWA
PENNSYLVANIA
NEW JERSEY
Chicago
Trenton
Harrisburg
OHIO
Baltimore
MARYLAND
Des Moines
Annapolis
Dover
DELAWARE
INDIANA
ILLINOIS
Columbus
WEST VIRGINIA
Washington, DC
Lincoln
Indianapolis
Springfield
Richmond
Topeka
MISSOURI
Charleston
VIRGINIA
Ohio River
Frankfort
Jefferson City
KENTUCKY
Raleigh
STATES
NORTH CAROLINA
OKLAHOMA
Nashville
TENNESSEE
Oklahoma City
Columbia
ARKANSAS
Memphis
Little Rock
SOUTH CAROLINA
Atlanta
ALABAMA
ATLANTIC OCEAN
MISSISSIPPI
GEORGIA
Dallas
Montgomery
LOUISIANA
Jackson
Tallahassee
Baton Rouge
Austin
FLORIDA
Houston
San Antonio
Gulf of Mexico
Kilometers 0
500
SCALE
Miles 0
500
95°
90°
85°
80°
75°
70°
65°
45°
40°
35°
30°
25°

CHAPTER 1

WHAT IS A GLOBE?

Lesson 1: Globes and Earth

NEW WORDS

globe

continent

ocean

This is a book about people and places. In it, you will meet many interesting people. You will visit many interesting places. Each of these places is a different part of Earth. To find the places, you will learn about globes and maps.

A girl named Lynda Rosen wrote a letter to a pen pal. Here is how she addressed the envelope:

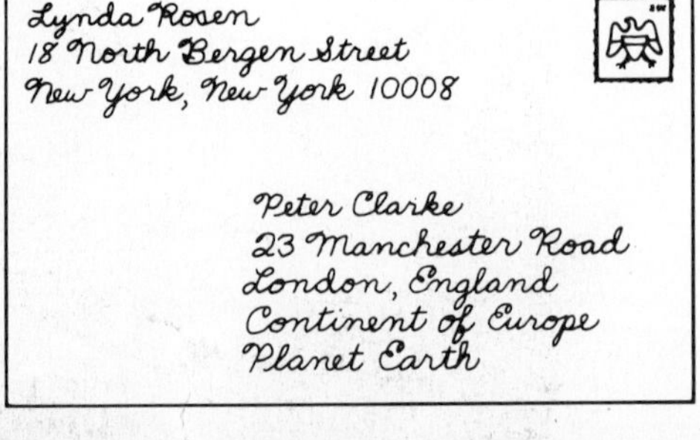

Lynda Rosen
18 North Bergen Street
New York, New York 10008

Peter Clarke
23 Manchester Road
London, England
Continent of Europe
Planet Earth

Of course, Lynda did not need to name all those places. Everyone lives on Earth. At least, right now everyone does. The workers in the United States Postal Service know that. They also know that England is in Europe. But suppose *you* had to deliver the letter. You might have some questions. What is a continent? Where is Europe? How can people find places on Earth?

On page 14 is a photograph of Earth. It was taken by astronauts far out in space. The Earth is seen from the moon. Notice that Earth is round. Parts of Earth are covered with white clouds. Water is blue. The land looks brown.

Below is a model of Earth. It is called a **globe.** A globe is round like Earth. On a globe, there are no clouds. You can see land more clearly. It is easy to tell what parts of Earth are covered with water.

On page 16 are drawings of both sides of a globe. There are seven large areas of land on Earth. They are called **continents.** The names of

This globe shows North America and South America.

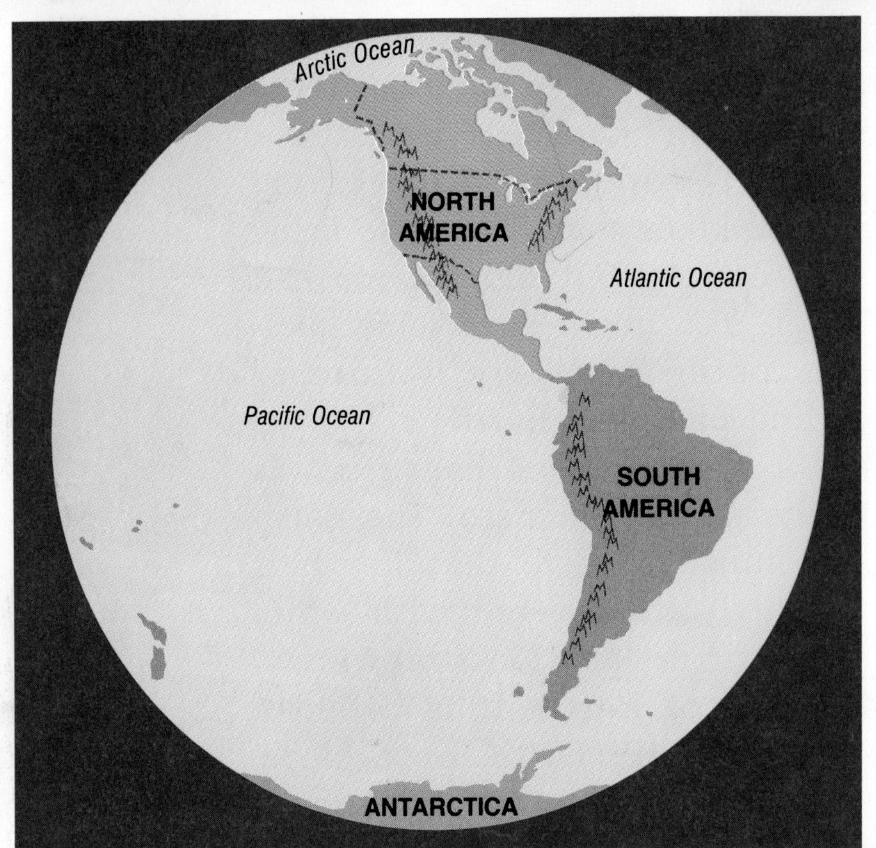
Arctic Ocean
NORTH
AMERICA
Atlantic Ocean
Pacific Ocean
SOUTH
AMERICA
ANTARCTICA

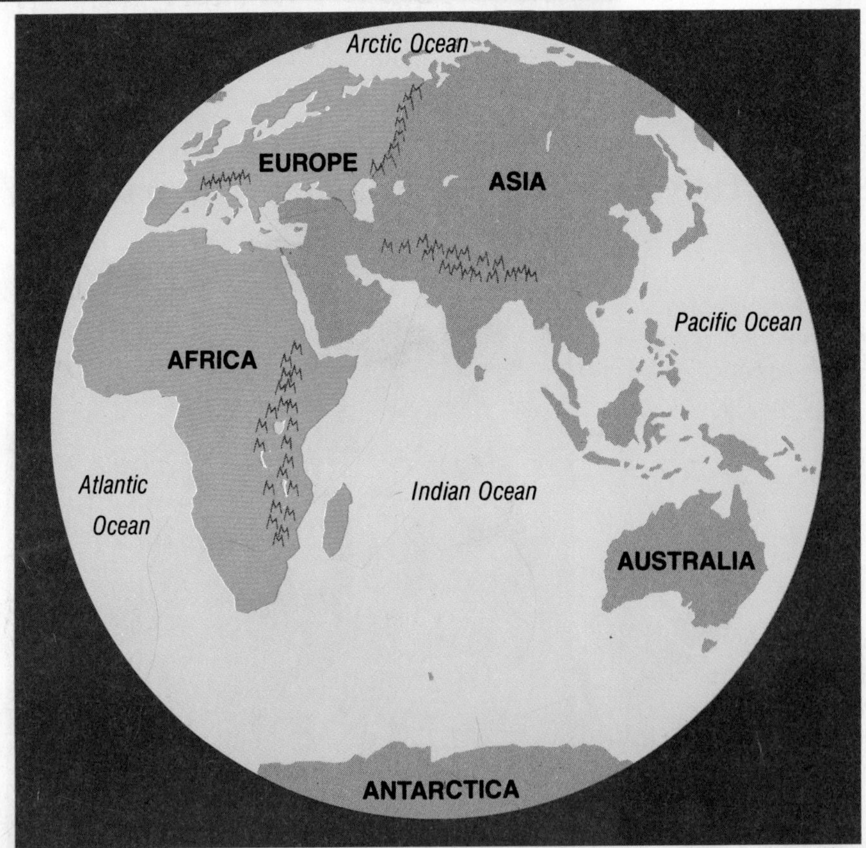
Arctic Ocean
EUROPE
ASIA
AFRICA
Pacific Ocean
Atlantic
Ocean
Indian Ocean
AUSTRALIA
ANTARCTICA

FUN FACTS

When you mail a letter, you put it in an envelope. It's easy to do because you can buy paper and envelopes almost everywhere. But what do you think it was like for people long ago?

Thousands of years ago, one group of people wrote their letters on clay tablets. After writing the letter, they wrapped thin sheets of clay around it. Then they pressed the edges and put it in the oven to bake. Baking hardened the clay. This thin clay covering was their envelope.

A sack full of these letters would be quite a load for a mail carrier! But few letters were sent in those days. Few people could read or write. So the mail carrier had only one letter to deliver at a time.

the continents are on the drawings. You live on the continent of North America. Lynda's friend lives on the continent of Europe.

There are also four great oceans on Earth. **Oceans** are very large bodies of water. Most of Earth is covered by oceans. Look at the globes. Name the four oceans.

REVIEW

WATCH YOUR WORDS

1. A(n) ___ is a large area of land on Earth.
   ocean globe continent
2. A(n)___is a model of Earth.
   ocean globe continent

CHECK YOUR FACTS

Look at the Globes

3. Name the seven continents.
4. What two continents are not connected to any others?
5. Which continent seems to be the largest?

THINK ABOUT IT

Two of the continents look like one large land area. Some people think of these two as one huge continent. Which two are they? What name can you think of for this huge continent?

Lesson 2: Which Way Are North and South?

NEW WORDS

- direction
- North Pole
- South Pole
- north
- south

The globe on the next page shows the continent of North America. Three nations take up most of the land on the continent. They are Canada, the United States, and Mexico.

Look at the globe. On this globe, north is at or toward the top. South is at or toward the bottom of the globe. North and south are both directions. A **direction** is a line along which you are facing, pointing, or moving. We use directions to help find places on a globe. We also use directions to tell people how to get someplace.

The place that is farthest north on Earth is called the **North Pole.** The place that is farthest south is the **South Pole.** Look at the globe. Pretend you are standing at the North Pole. Every place on Earth will be south of you. Then pretend you are standing at the South Pole. Every place will be north of you.

Here is a way to remember north and south. Suppose a place is closer to the North Pole than you are. Then it is **north** of you. Suppose it is closer to the South Pole than you are. Then it is **south** of you.

North America is closer to the North Pole than it is to the South Pole. It is closer to the North Pole than South America is. That is why it is called *North* America. The United States is in the middle of North America. It is closer to the North Pole than Mexico is. It is north of Mexico.

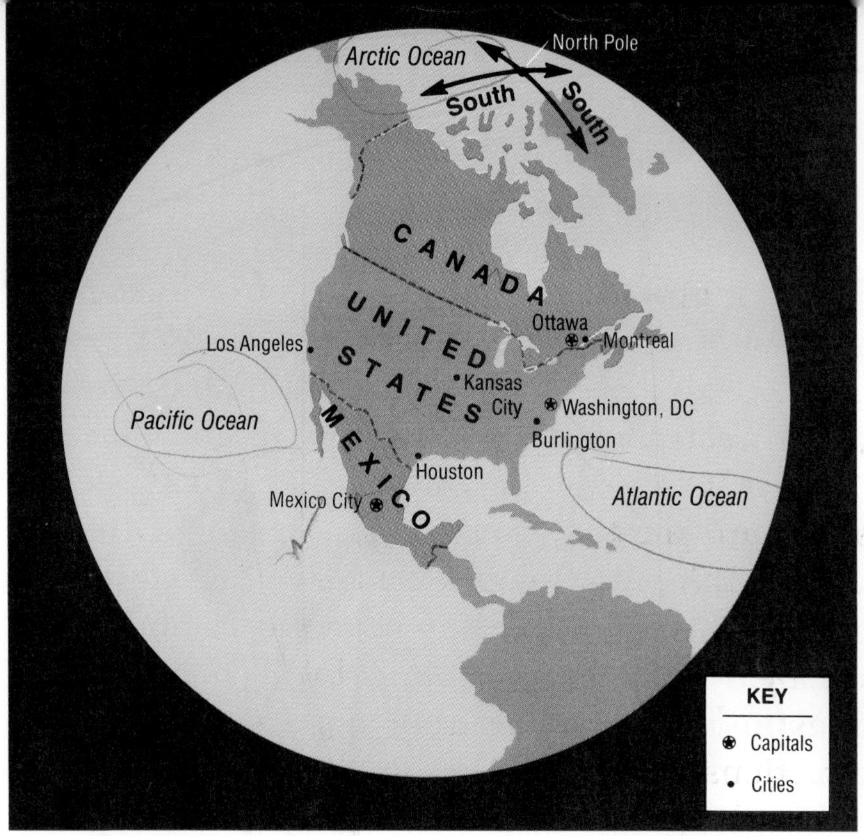

The United States is closer to the South Pole than Canada is. It is south of Canada.

REVIEW

WATCH YOUR WORDS

1. North and south are___.
   directions poles continents
2. The direction toward the top of a globe is___.
   North Pole north south
3. The place on Earth that is farthest south is the___.
   North Pole direction
   South Pole

CHECK YOUR FACTS

Look at the Globe

4. Is Canada north or south of Mexico?
5. Is Mexico City north or south of Montreal?

THINK ABOUT IT

One part of the United States is north of much of Canada. Name it if you can.

Lesson 3: Which Way Are East and West?

NEW WORDS

east

west

cardinal directions

You have learned about the directions north and south. There are two other directions on a globe. They are called **east** and **west.** North, south, east, and west can help you find places.

Look at the globe on page 21. Suppose you were going from the Atlantic Ocean to the Pacific Ocean. You would be traveling west. The part of the United States near the Pacific Ocean is called the West.

Suppose you went from the Pacific Ocean to the Atlantic Ocean. You would be traveling east. The part of the United States near the Atlantic Ocean is called the East.

You can find east and west by watching the sunrise and sunset. In the morning, the sun seems to rise in the east. In the evening, the sun seems to set in the west. Find out where east and west are in your school.

There is another way to find east and west. When you face north, east is on your right side. West is on your left side. When you face south, it is the other way around. East is on your left side. West is on your right side.

Look at the globe once again. Suppose you were taking a trip around the world. You could travel all the way around the world going east. Or you could travel all the way around going west. Explain how you could always be going either east or west.

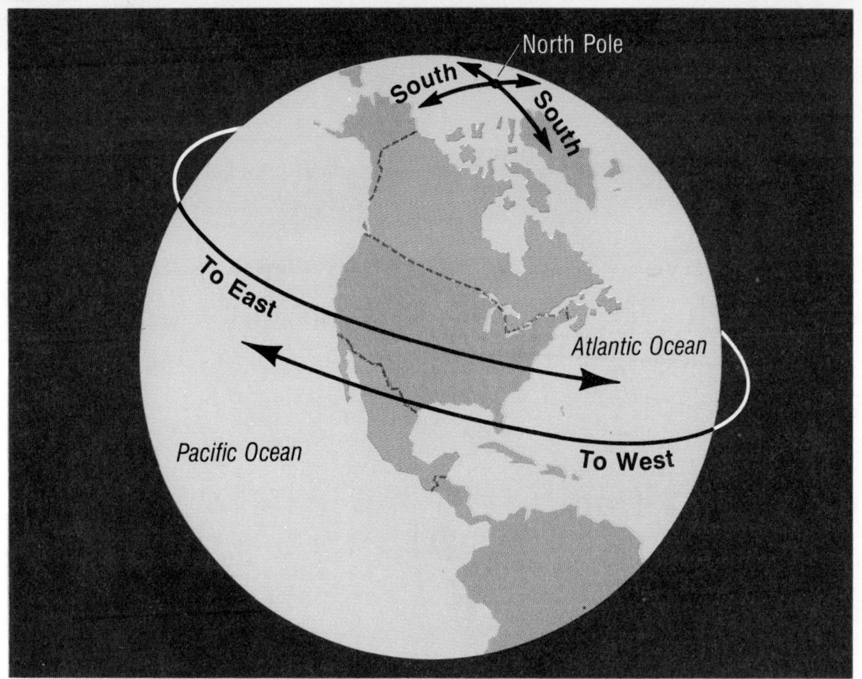

North, south, east, and west are called the **cardinal directions.** The word *cardinal* means "most important." The cardinal directions are the four main directions on Earth. People use these directions to find places.

REVIEW

WATCH YOUR WORDS

1. ___ is the direction toward the sunrise.
   East West South
2. ___ is the direction toward the sunset.
   East West North

CHECK YOUR FACTS

3. What are the names of the four cardinal directions?
4. What is the area of the United States near the Pacific Ocean called?
5. If you face north, what direction is to your right?

THINK ABOUT IT

Stand facing west. What direction is to your left? What direction is to your right? What direction is behind you?

CHAPTER REVIEW

WATCH YOUR WORDS

1. A___is a model of Earth.
continent globe direction
2. East is a___.
continent globe direction
3. A(n)___is a large land area.
continent globe ocean
4. The ___ is at the "top" of the Earth.
South Pole North Pole continent
5. We see the sunset in the___.
north east west

CHECK YOUR FACTS

6. Where does everyone live right now?
7. How is a globe like Earth?
8. How many continents are there?
9. Name the four oceans.
10. What three nations take up most of North America?
11. How do we use directions?
12. What place on Earth is farthest north?
13. What is the part of the United States near the Atlantic Ocean called?
14. Where does the sun seem to rise?
15. What are the names of the four cardinal directions?

USE YOUR GLOBES

16. Look at the globes on page 16 to answer these questions. Suppose you are in South America. You want to get to North America. In what direction will you go?
17. Suppose you are in Europe. What continent is to the south of you?
18. Suppose you are in Africa. What ocean will you cross to get to Australia?
19. What continent is the farthest south?
20. What ocean surrounds the North Pole?

THINK ABOUT IT

21. Are continents the only land areas on Earth?
22. Does there seem to be more land or more water on Earth?
23. What would happen if you kept traveling north in a straight line?
24. What would happen if you kept traveling west in a straight line?
25. Suppose you are lost in the woods in the early morning. How can you tell which way is east?

CHAPTER 2 PEOPLE AND PLACES

Lesson 1: Communities Are Places

People live on much of Earth's land. Most people live in communities. **Communities** are places where people can get the things they need and want. Most communities in the United States have homes, schools, and stores.

NEW WORD

community

Communities have places for all the things that people do. They have places where people live and work. They have places where people learn and pray. They have places where people can get help. They have many places where people play. These are the ways that communities are alike.

Communities are different in many ways, too. They are of different sizes. They are in different places. People in different communities may live in different ways.

This is a big city seen from an airplane.

This picture shows a small town.

Communities can be big or small. They can have many buildings or only a few. They can be near a river or an ocean. They can be surrounded by dry land. They can be in hot lands or cold lands. They can be on land that is high or low. But a community always has people. It is a place where people live, work, and play.

This town is on the sea.

This community is in a dry land.

REVIEW

CHECK YOUR FACTS

1. What is a community?
2. What kinds of places do communities have?
3. Name three ways in which communities can be different from one another.
4. A neighborhood (can/cannot) be a community.
5. What does a community always have?

THINK ABOUT IT

What is the name of your community?

Lesson 2: Cities Are Special Communities

NEW WORDS

- city
- population
- area
- occupation

A **city** is a special kind of community. There are four special things about a city.

A city is a place with a large population (POP yuh LAY shun). The **population** is the number of people who live in a place. A large population is the first special thing about a city. A big city may have millions of people. A small city may have only 20,000 people.

There is a second special thing about a city. It has a large **area**. That is the amount of land the city covers. A city takes up a lot of land.

Cities are crowded. That is the third thing that makes cities special. In big cities, there are thousands and thousands of buildings. The buildings are very close together. Many people live, work, or shop in each building. All these people use the streets and sidewalks. They use the parks and playgrounds.

People crowd a busy city street.

This man works in a city factory. He puts together electric equipment.

The people in cities work at many different kinds of jobs. The jobs people do are called **occupations** (OK yuh PAY shunz). The many different occupations are the fourth thing that makes cities special. Some city occupations are grocer, factory worker, police officer, and fire fighter.

People live in cities because there are many places to work. In cities there are many ways for people to get what they need.

REVIEW

WATCH YOUR WORDS

1. The number of people who live in a place is its___.
area population crowd

2. The amount of land a community covers is its___.
area population place

CHECK YOUR FACTS

3. Name four special things about a city.

4. What is another word for the jobs people do?

5. Name three jobs people do in cities.

THINK ABOUT IT

6. What is the biggest city near your community?

TRY SOMETHING NEW

7. Find out the population of your community.

Lesson 3: Groups of Communities Form Urban Areas

Sometimes, communities are very close to one another. Often, a large city is surrounded by many small communities. Small communities near a city are called **suburbs**. A city and its suburbs make up an **urban area**. This is a large area where many people live.

NEW WORDS

suburb
urban area
chart
bar graph

A map is a drawing. It can show the whole Earth or part of it. This map shows the large urban areas of the United States. At least a million people live in each of these areas. One urban area has more than 9 million people. This is the urban area around New York City. Can you find it on the map?

URBAN AREAS OF THE UNITED STATES

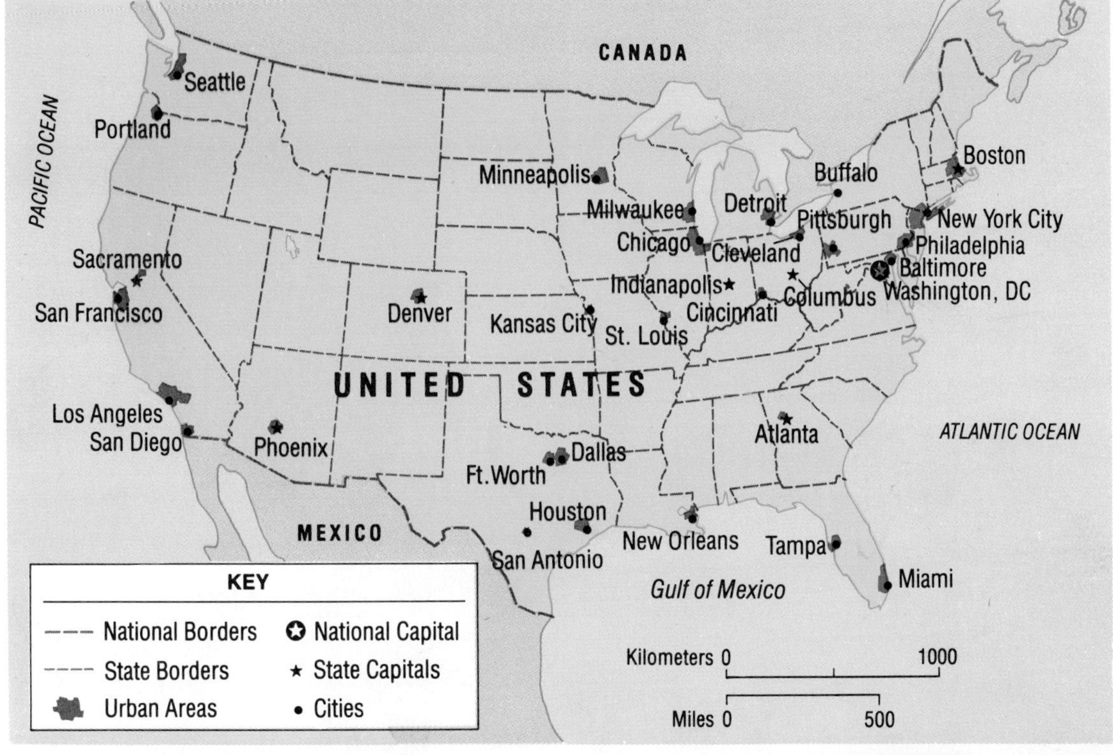

A **chart** is a list of facts, such as numbers. It shows these facts in order. A chart can help you find and remember facts. Charts can show how many people live in places such as urban areas.

Here is a chart of the 10 largest urban areas in the United States. This chart tells you how many people live in each area. But you cannot

U.S. URBAN AREAS

Urban Area	Number of people	Urban Area	Number of people
New York City	9,100,000	San Francisco	3,200,000
Los Angeles	7,400,000	Washington, DC	3,000,000
Chicago	7,100,000	Dallas - Fort Worth	3,000,000
Philadelphia	4,700,000	Houston	2,900,000
Detroit	4,300,000	Boston	2,800,000

POPULATION GRAPH - URBAN AREAS

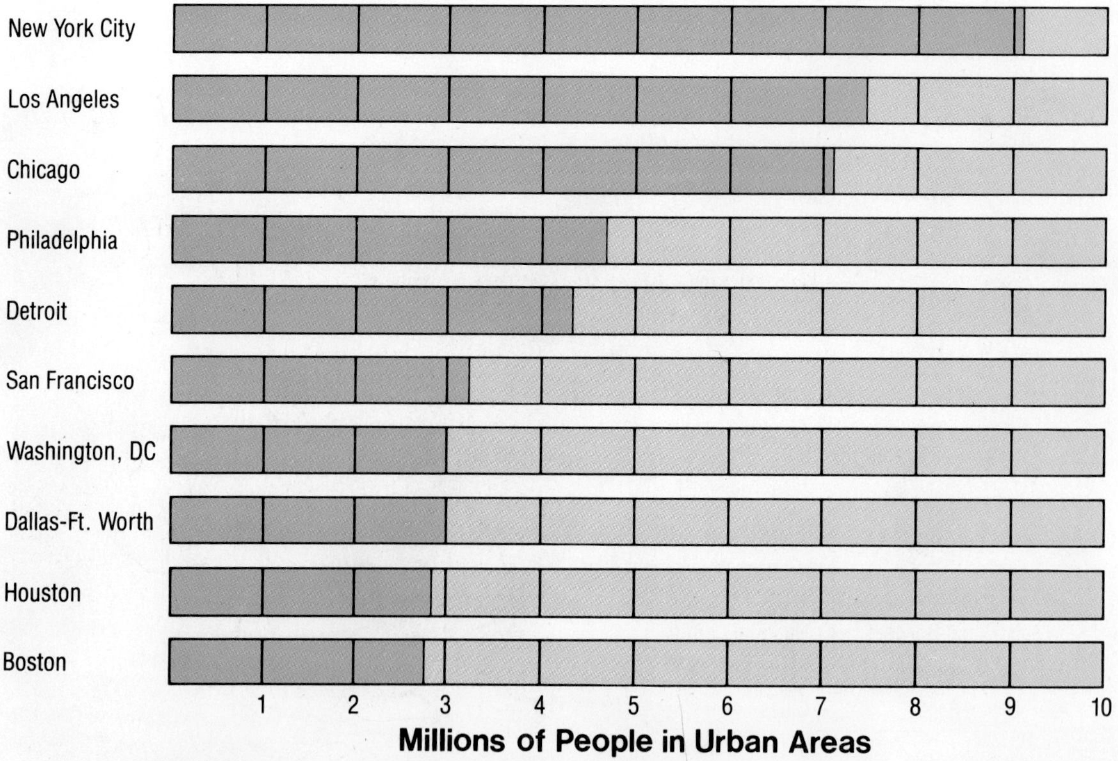

New York City
Los Angeles
Chicago
Philadelphia
Detroit
San Francisco
Washington, DC
Dallas-Ft. Worth
Houston
Boston

1 2 3 4 5 6 7 8 9 10

Millions of People in Urban Areas

see where the urban areas are. That is one difference between a map and a chart.

There is another way to show how many people live in an urban area. It is called a **bar graph**. This is a picture in which symbols are used to show facts. Here is how it works:

Suppose this ▭ stands for 1 million people. One million people = ▭. How would we show 2 million people?

Two million people would = ▭▭ . How would we show 3 million people? How about 10 million people?

On page 28 is a bar graph. It shows the urban areas on the map and chart. The bar graph has a title to tell what it is about. The names of the urban areas are on the side. The numbers of people go across the bottom. Another label tells what the numbers mean.

REVIEW

CHECK YOUR FACTS

Look at the Bar Graph

1. Which of these urban areas has more people, Los Angeles or Chicago?
2. About how many people are there in the Philadelphia urban area?

Look at the Lesson

3. What makes up an urban area?
4. What can a chart tell you about urban areas?
5. What do we use to show facts in a bar graph?

TRY SOMETHING NEW

Keep a record for the next 7 days. Write down the amount of time you spend on homework every day. At the end of the 7 days, make a bar graph. Show the time you have spent each day doing homework.

Lesson 4: People's Needs

NEW WORD

need

Each person in a community has needs. **Needs** are things people must have to live, be healthy, or be happy. All people have the same needs. These needs fit into three big groups:

People need to stay alive and healthy.
People need to feel safe.
People need to feel good about themselves.

People need air, water, and food to stay alive. Most people can go for about 4 weeks without food. They can go for about 4 days without water. But they can go for only a few minutes without air. People need to eat the right kinds of foods to stay healthy. They also need clothes and homes to protect them. Clothes protect people from the hot sun as well as from the cold. Homes give people shelter from the weather. They also keep people safe.

Good food keeps people healthy.

Clothing keeps our bodies warm.

Other people make us feel safe.

People need to feel safe. This is the second big need. They need safe places to go to. They need other people they can trust. They need to be able to live and work without being afraid.

People need to feel good about themselves. This is the third big need. Each person needs to be able to say: "I'm OK. I like being me. I am a good person." People need to learn how to take care of themselves. They feel good when they can do things on their own.

People in communities help one another fill important needs. That is a reason people live in communities.

REVIEW

CHECK YOUR FACTS

1. What are needs?
2. List the three big groups of needs.
3. Name three things people need to stay alive.
4. Name two things people need to feel safe.
5. What things make you feel good about yourself?

THINK ABOUT IT

Tell how some of your needs have been filled today.

Lesson 5: Needs and Communities

NEW WORD

depend

Many people help you fill your needs. Your family helps you get food and clothing. Parents and friends help you feel safe. Your teachers can help you feel good about yourself.

There are many other people who help you, too. Police officers help keep the community safe. But police officers cannot grow all their own food. They cannot build their own homes and keep them warm. They cannot make their own clothes. They need other people to help them with these things.

Sometimes, police officers get sick. They need doctors. They cannot teach their children everything the children need to know. Police officers depend on other people to help them. People **depend** on other people when they count on them.

Everyone in a community depends on everyone else. People count on other people to do a

A woman buys food at an outdoor market.

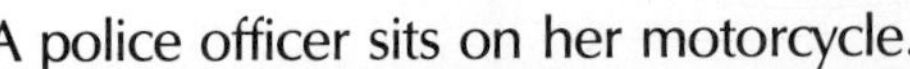

A police officer sits on her motorcycle.

FUN FACTS

We count on the police to keep our communities safe. But police forces have been around for less than 200 years. In the old days, groups of people had the duty of catching thieves. There were no regular police officers on duty all the time.

The first police force was started in London, England, in 1829. These police officers wore blue uniforms. They carried rattles that they used to call for help. The only weapon they carried was a club called a police officer. That's right, the name *police officer* comes from the club they carried.

New York had the first police in the United States. The New York police also carried clubs. Other cities soon started their own police forces. Our police did not carry guns until years later. London police carry clubs to this day.

job. This is the most important reason people live in communities. They need other people. They depend on other people.

Different people have different jobs in the community. Each job fills a need.

REVIEW

CHECK YOUR FACTS

1. Name some people who help fill your needs.
2. What does a police officer do?
3. What does it mean to say that people depend on each other?
4. Give an important reason people live in communities.
5. What does each job in a community do?

THINK ABOUT IT

Name some people you have never met who help fill your needs. An example might be a fire fighter. A fire fighter helps keep your community safe from fire.

CHAPTER REVIEW

WATCH YOUR WORDS

1. ___ are places where people can get what they need.
   Communities Populations Areas
2. ___ are the jobs people do.
   Communities Populations Occupations
3. A(n) ___ is a smaller community near a city.
   urban area suburb occupation
4. A ___ is a picture in which symbols are used to show facts.
   continent direction bar graph
5. The ___ of a place is the number of people who live there.
   area population direction

CHECK YOUR FACTS

6. Most people (do/do not) live in communities.
7. All communities (do/do not) have places for the things people do.
8. A city is a community with a (large/small) population.
9. A city has a (large/small) area.
10. In cities, people are (crowded together/spread out).
11. People in cities have (many/few) kinds of jobs.
12. What is an urban area made up of?
13. Everyone has (the same/different) kinds of needs.
14. What are the three main kinds of needs?
15. Name two jobs that fill people's needs.

USE YOUR MAP, CHART, AND BAR GRAPH

16. Look at the map of the United States on page 27. Are there more urban areas in the east or the west? In the north or the south?
17. Look at the chart of urban areas on page 28. What is the second-largest urban area?
18. Look at both the map and the chart. Is the capital of the United States a large urban area?
19. Look at the bar graph on page 28. Is the largest urban area more than twice as large as the smallest?
20. Look at the bar graph again. About how many people are in the Chicago urban area?

TRY SOMETHING NEW

21. Name at least two different kinds of places in your community. Tell what need each place fills.
22. Make a scrapbook of pictures from newspapers and magazines. Put in pictures that show people filling needs.

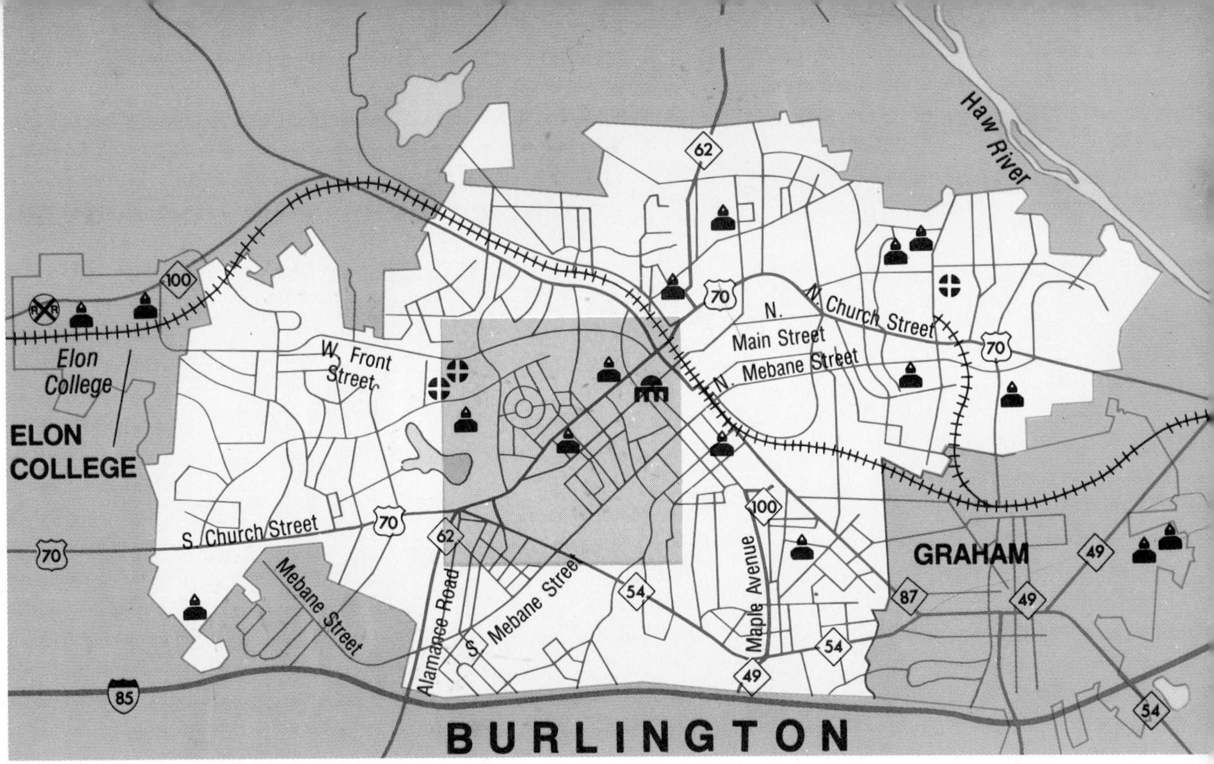

CHAPTER 3 MAPPING A COMMUNITY

Lesson 1: Exploring a Community

NEW WORDS

- **photograph**
- **aerial photograph**

How can we explore a community? We can go there. We can look at the buildings. We can walk up and down the streets. We can look around the corners. We can look for places to play. This is one way to explore a community.

Visiting a community takes time and a lot of traveling. There is an easier way. We can learn about a community without going there.

On the next page is a **photograph** (FOH tuh GRAF). It is a picture of part of a community.

This community is called Burlington. It is in the state of North Carolina. The photograph was taken from an airplane flying over the community. For this reason, it is called an **aerial** (AR ee ul) **photograph.** *Aerial* means "in or from the air."

Houses look tiny in this aerial photograph of Burlington, North Carolina.

Look at the photograph. Long lines are mostly streets. Dark areas are trees. Small square shapes are mostly buildings. Very light areas are mostly open fields.

FUN FACTS

North Carolina has miles of beautiful beaches along the Atlantic Ocean. In the summer, people come there to swim. Years ago, in the winter of 1903, two brothers came to a place called Kitty Hawk. They made history there.

The brothers were Orville and Wilbur Wright. With them they brought an airplane they had built. One sunny day in December, they made the first successful airplane flight ever.

The Wright brothers' plane had wings on two levels. The pilot flew the plane lying down on the bottom wing.

Wilbur and Orville flipped a coin to see who would try to fly the plane first. Orville won. Wilbur ran next to the plane to help keep the wings steady. The plane gained speed and took off!

The first flight lasted only 12 seconds. The plane flew only 120 feet (37 meters). But the age of the airplane had begun.

REVIEW

CHECK YOUR FACTS

Look at the Lesson

1. Name two ways of learning things about a community.
2. The community in the photograph is called Burlington. What state is it in?
3. How is an aerial photograph taken?

Look at the Picture

4. There is an area of large buildings at the (upper right/ center) of the photograph.

TRY SOMETHING NEW

Ask your Chamber of Commerce if you can get an aerial photograph of your community.

Lesson 2: Learning from a Map

NEW WORDS

- map
- mapmaker
- symbol

You can find out a lot about a community from a photograph. But sometimes you want to know more about a place than a picture can show. A map can help you. As you know, a **map** is a drawing of Earth or a part of Earth. The map on page 39 shows all of Burlington. It shows you many things about the land around Burlington.

People who draw maps are called **mapmakers.** Mapmakers use little pictures to show you where things are on the map.

— shows you where main highways are.
shows you where schools are.
shows you where hospitals are. 
shows you where airports are.

These little pictures are called symbols. A **symbol** stands for a real thing. Symbols make maps easier to read.

Look on the map for a group of symbols. The mapmaker has placed them in a box. This box is called the key to the map. The key tells you what the symbols mean. To find out where the schools are, first look at the key. Find the symbol for schools. Now find the symbols on the map. They tell you where the schools are. How many schools are on the map?

Find the symbol for hospitals. Tell how many hospitals are on the map.

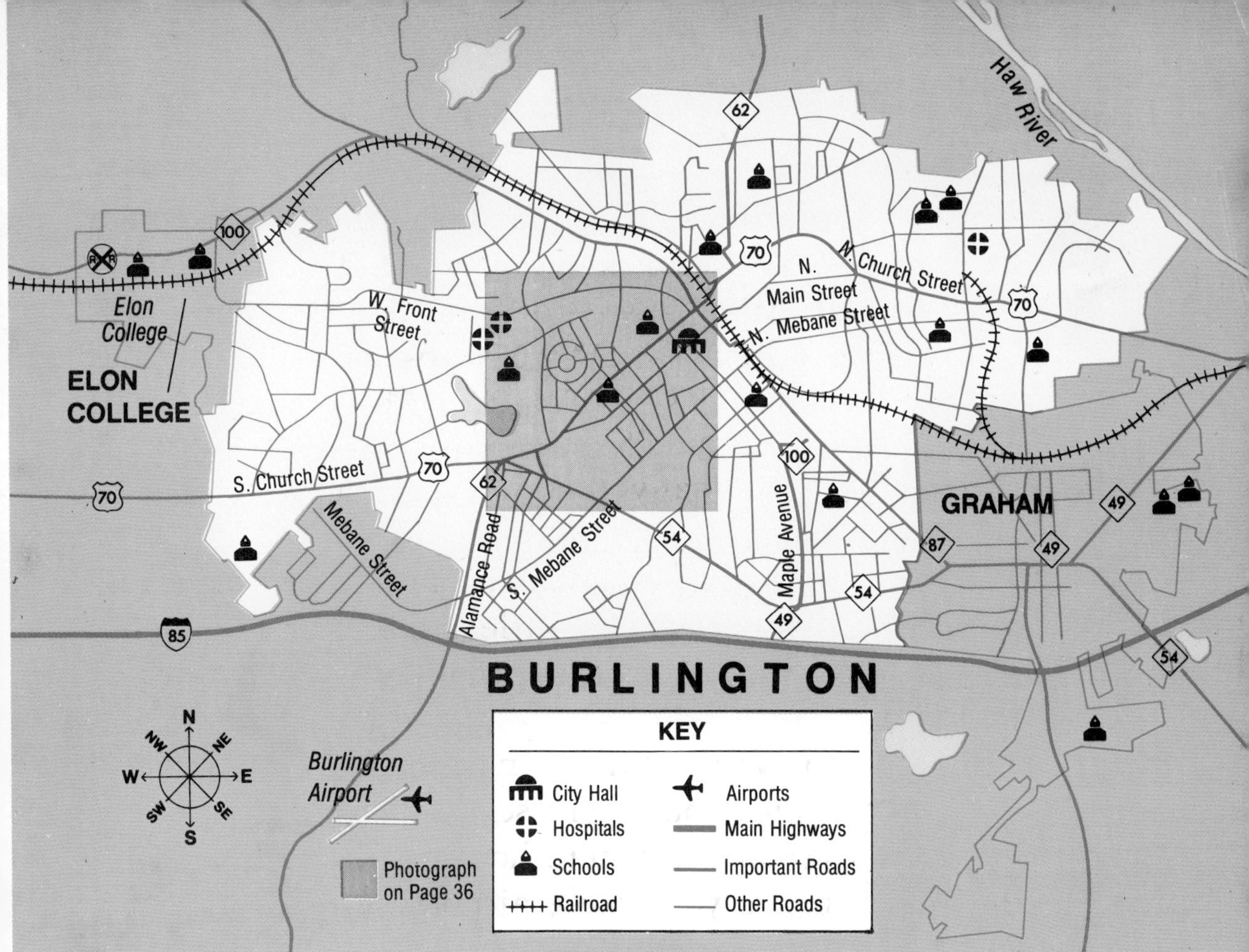

REVIEW

WATCH YOUR WORDS

1. A ___ is a picture that stands for something real.
   direction symbol key
2. A ___ tells you what symbols mean.
   map photograph key
3. A ___ is a drawing of Earth or a part of Earth.
   map symbol key

CHECK YOUR FACTS

Look at the Map

4. What is the number of the main highway that runs near Burlington?
5. City hall is (near/far from) the railroad.

TRY SOMETHING NEW

Draw a map of your neighborhood. Use symbols and a key.

Lesson 3: Finding Places on a Map

NEW WORD

grid

Sometimes, it is hard to find places on a map. You do not know what part of the map to look at. Mapmakers help you find places by putting a grid on the map. A **grid** is made by lines that cross the map. These lines make small squares all over the map. There are letters across the top and the bottom. There are numbers down one or both sides.

Each square has both a letter and a number. These can help you find what you are looking for. Suppose you want to find a place. You must know the letter and number of the square the place is in.

Suppose you wanted to find city hall. Without the grid, this might be hard to do. But suppose you know that city hall is in square *C2*. Then city hall is easy to find. Look at the top of the map. Find the letter *C*. Notice that it is between two lines that go up and down. The space between those two lines is called *C*.

Now, look at the edge of the map. Find the number *2*. Notice that it is between two lines that go across the map. The space between those two lines is called *2*.

Move one finger down the *C* space. At the same time, move one finger across the *2* space. City hall is in the square where *C* and *2* meet.

You can use the grid to help other people find places on the map. Find the square on the map that has Elon College in it. Then find the letter

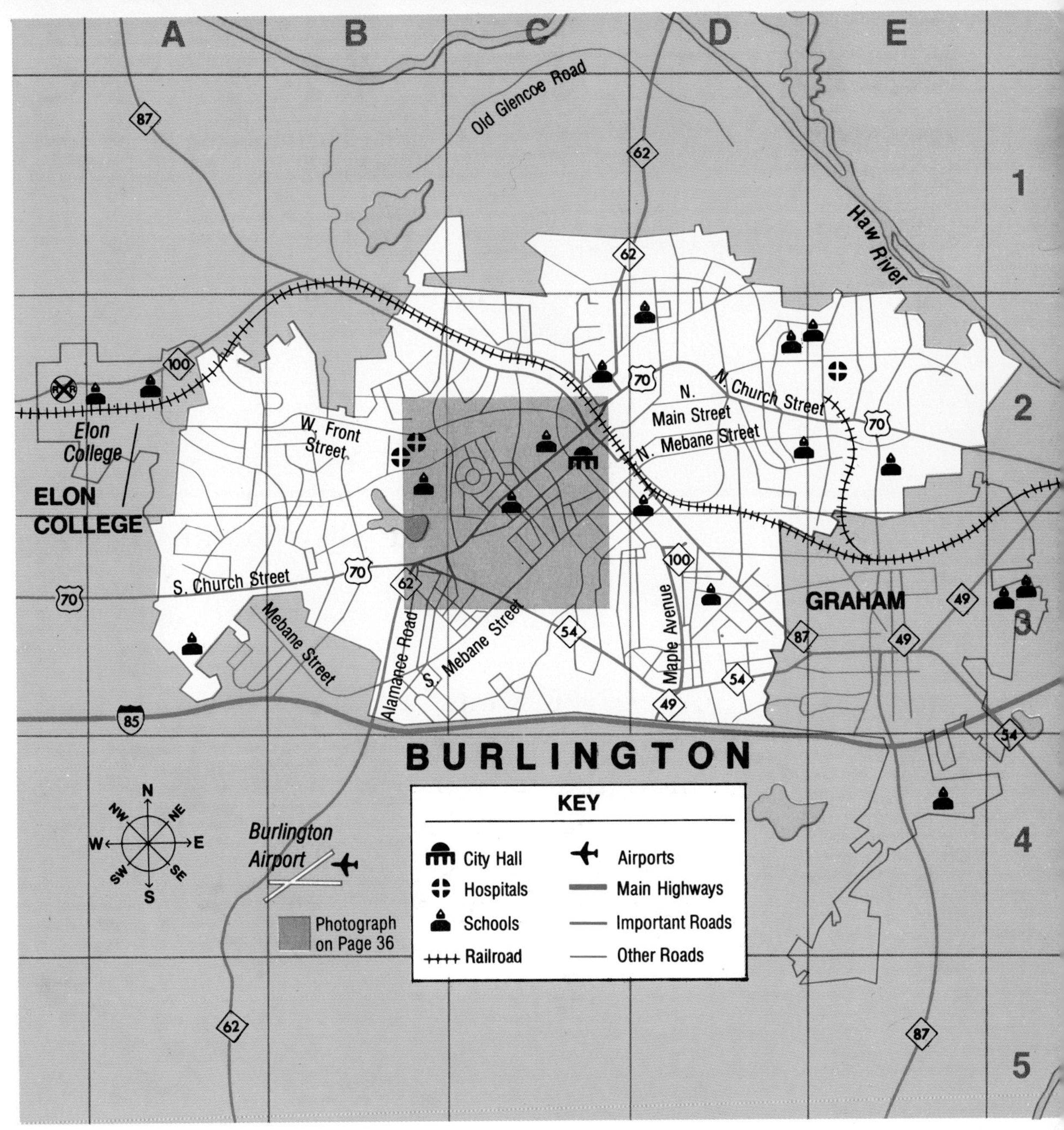

of the square at the top of the map. Find the number of the square at the edge of the map. Suppose someone asks you where Elon College is on the map. You can answer by giving the number and letter of the square.

REVIEW

CHECK YOUR FACTS

Look at the Map

1. What important place is in square *B4*?
2. What square is most of the town of Graham in?
3. What square has two hospitals in it?
4. What square has the most schools?
5. Name an important road in square *D3*.
6. In what square does the main railroad line branch off?

THINK ABOUT IT

Suppose you lived in Burlington on North Mebane Street. What roads might you take to get to the airport?

Lesson 4: The Eastern United States

NEW WORDS

- government
- nation
- country
- state
- border
- capital
- mountain
- mountain range

We have been studying maps of Burlington. Burlington is in the state of North Carolina. North Carolina is part of our nation. Our nation is the United States of America. It is on the continent of North America. Before we go on, we should find out what some words mean. What is a state? What is a nation?

A nation is also called a country. A nation has its own land. It has its own people. A special group of people makes rules and laws for the nation. This group is called the **government.** Thus, a **nation** is a group of people with their own government and their own land. A **country** is the same thing.

A **state** is a part of our nation. Our nation is divided into 50 states. States have their own land, people, and government.

The map on page 44 shows the Eastern United States. There are many symbols on the map. Special lines show borders. They look like this – – –. A **border** divides one area from another. The borders on the map show where one state ends and another state begins.

Each state has a capital. A **capital** is a city where the government is located. State governments are located in state capitals. On this map, the symbol for a state capital is ★ . Also find the symbol for our nation's capital on the map. Our nation's capital is Washington, DC. It is the city where our nation's government is located.

Burlington, North Carolina, is located in the eastern part of our country. Look at the map again. It shows just the eastern part of our country. This area is located between the Atlantic Ocean and the Appalachian (AP uh LAY chun) Mountains. A **mountain** is an area of land much higher than the land around it. A **mountain range** is a group or row of mountains. The Appalachians are a mountain range.

This mountain is part of the Appalachian Mountain range in New York State.

THE EASTERN UNITED STATES

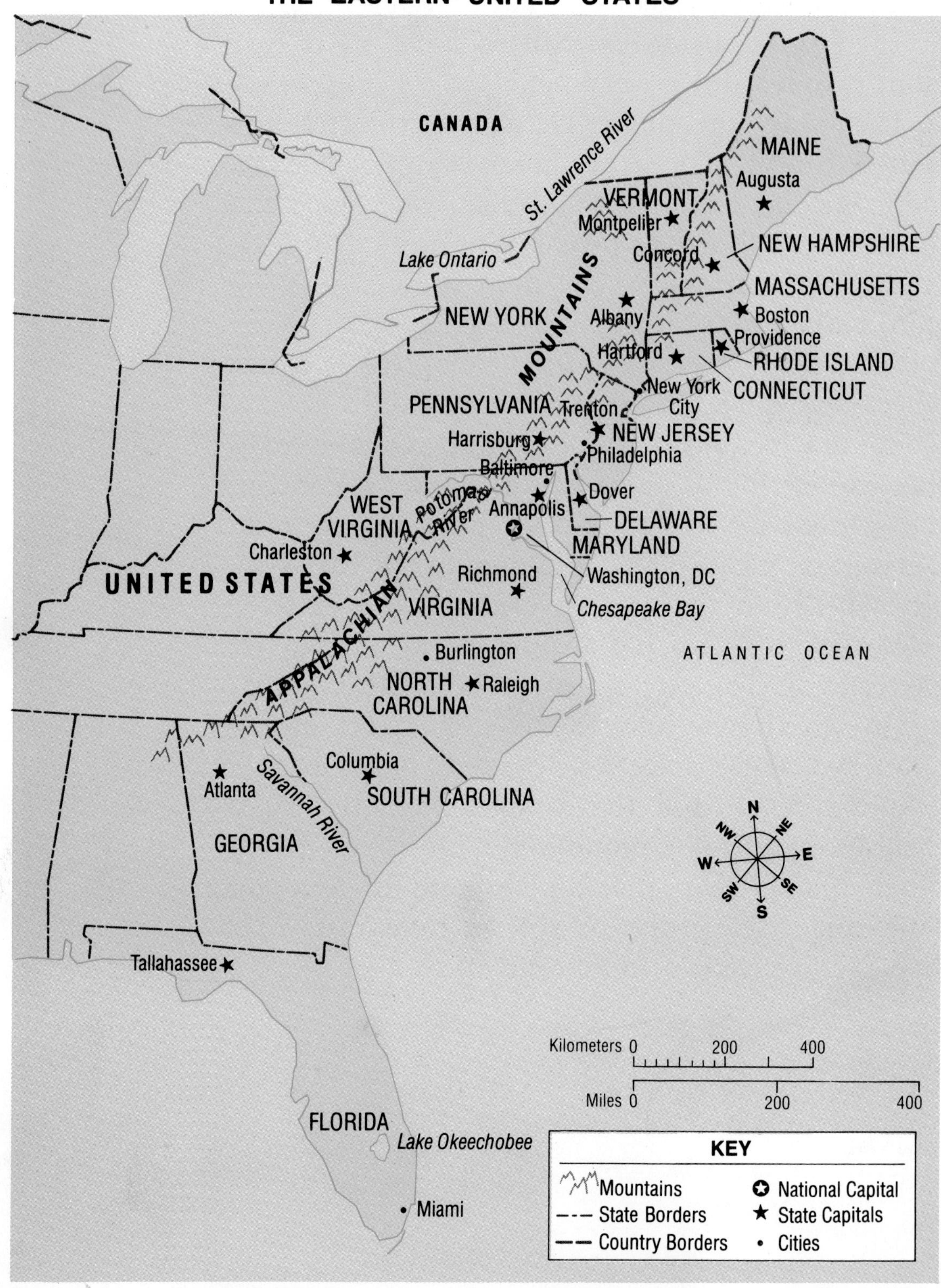

Seventeen states are located in the eastern part of our country. Rhode Island and Delaware are very small states. Study the map. There are many large cities in the east. Find New York City, Boston, and Philadelphia. Find Baltimore, Atlanta, and Miami. Name the state where each city is found. Tell how these cities are shown on the map. Do you live in any of these states? Try to learn from the map. Which states touch the Atlantic Ocean? Which states do not? Which eastern state is the farthest north? Which eastern state is the farthest south?

REVIEW

WATCH YOUR WORDS

1. A ___ is the same thing as a country.
state capital nation

2. A ___ is a city where the government is located.
state capital border

3. A ___ divides one area from another.
government country border

4. The ___ makes the rules and laws for the nation.
government country state

5. A ___ is much higher than the land around it.
border capital mountain

CHECK YOUR FACTS

6. North Carolina is part of what nation?

7. On what continent is our nation found?

8. What three things does a nation have?

9. Where are state governments located?

10. What is the name of our nation's capital?

TRY SOMETHING NEW

Rhode Island is the smallest of the 50 states. However, it has the longest name of all the states. Use an encyclopedia to find the full name of Rhode Island.

CHAPTER REVIEW

WATCH YOUR WORDS

1. A(n) ___ photograph is taken from an airplane.
   aerial mountain grid
2. People who draw maps are called___.
   photographers governments mapmakers
3. Lines that cross a map form a ___.
   grid symbol key
4. A___is a part of our nation.
   continent country state
5. The Appalachians are a___.
   capital mountain range state

CHECK YOUR FACTS

6. We (can/cannot) learn much about a community without going there.
7. How do mapmakers show you where things are?
8. How can you find out what the symbols on a map mean?
9. What does a grid on a map help you do?
10. What group of people make the rules and laws for a nation?
11. On a map, what shows where one state ends and another state begins?
12. What is always located in a capital city?
13. The eastern part of our country is located between what two things?
14. Delaware is a (large/small) state.
15. How many states are there in our nation?

USE YOUR MAPS

16. Can you find out more things with an aerial photograph or with a map?
17. Look at the map of Burlington on page 39. What river flows near the city?
18. Look at the map of Burlington on page 41. In what square is most of Elon College located?
19. Look at the map of the Eastern United States on page 44. What other country is shown on the map?
20. Look at the map of the Eastern United States again. Between what states is Washington, DC?

THINK ABOUT IT

21. Do you think aerial photographs might be useful in making maps? Why, or why not?
22. Can there be maps of places other than Earth?
23. There are national governments and state governments. Can you think of another kind of government?

CHAPTER 4 THE HISTORY OF BURLINGTON

Lesson 1: Burlington's Time Line

People often tell the story of things that happened in the past. When they do this, they are telling history. **History** is the story of the past.

NEW WORDS

history

time line

All people and places have a history. Your community has a history. It is the story of the many things that happened there in the past. You have a history, too. Your history is the story of your life.

Everyone has a life story. Sometimes, people tell interesting stories about their lives. They may even tell about other peoples' lives. You have probably heard stories about the lives of some famous people.

Jenny is in the third grade. Jenny wanted to tell the story of her life. She knew it was quite a long story. So she decided to tell only some important things that happened to her. She drew a time line.

A **time line** is a line with important dates. A few words tell what happened on each date. This is a helpful way to show events in order.

Here is Jenny's time line.

Jenny's Time Line

1975	1978	1979	1981	1983
Born in Chicago	Family moved to new house	had tonsils out	started first grade	started third grade

Here is the time line Jenny's mother drew.

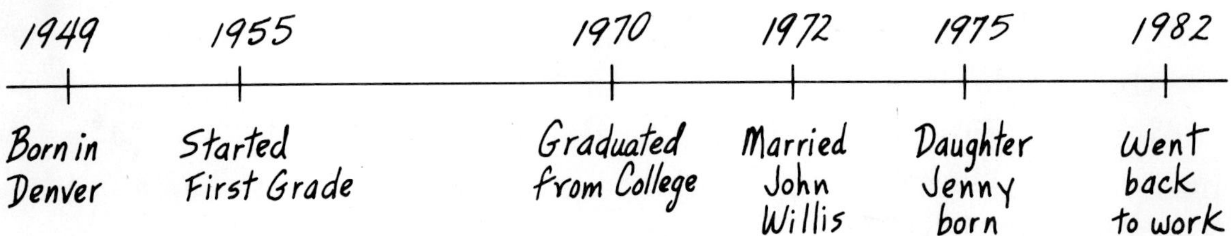

The time lines tell you a lot about Jenny and her mother. The time lines tell you when they were born. They tell you what events Jenny and her mother think are important. They show you that Jenny is part of her mother's history.

On the next page is a time line for Burlington. Each date tells you something important

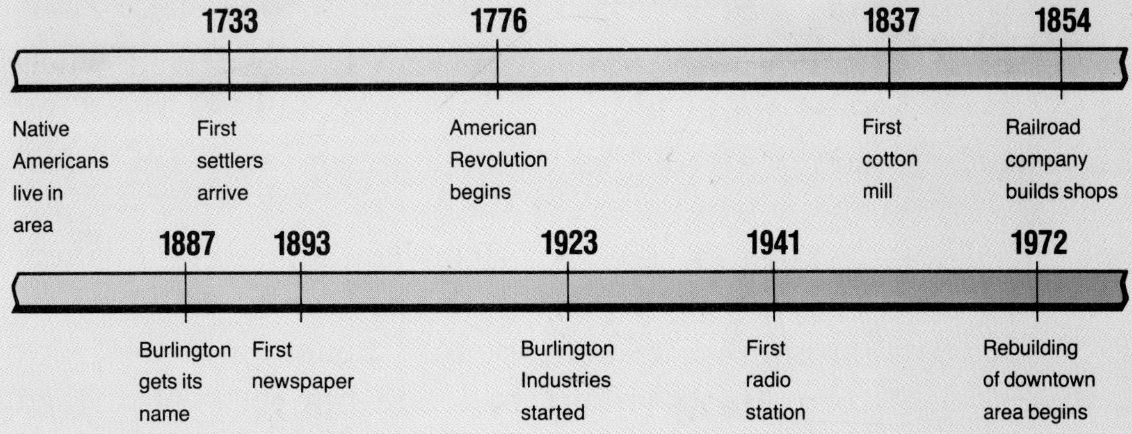

about this community. Read the time line with care. Do you now have an idea of how Burlington grew? Which of these events happened first: the first newspaper or the first radio station?

It would take a long time to learn all of Burlington's history. Each event on the time line has its own story. You will be reading some of these stories in the next few lessons.

REVIEW

CHECK YOUR FACTS

Look at the Lesson

1. All people and places (do/do not) have a history.
2. What is included in a time line?
3. What does the word *history* mean?

Look at the Time Line

4. Which came first, Burlington Industries or the first cotton mill?
5. What is the last event shown on Burlington's time line?

TRY SOMETHING NEW

Draw a time line of events in your own life.

Lesson 2: American Indian Times

NEW WORD

harvest

Long ago, only American Indians lived where Burlington is today. A man named Robert Lawson visited the American Indians. He wrote about what he saw.

Most of the American Indians were farmers. They lived in villages. They grew melons, cucumbers, squash, beans, peas, potatoes, and corn. Each village had one big farm. The farm went all around the village. The American Indians did not have fences. All the people knew their own parts of the farm. They did not take anyone else's food.

Every year, the American Indians had a big feast after the harvest in the fall. The **harvest** is the time the crops are gathered. They gave thanks to the Good Spirit for the good harvest. They would ask for another good year. People

Left: American Indians farm the land. *Right:* They prepare a harvest feast.

would walk on foot up to 3 days to join the feast. Then, they would buy and sell things. Our Thanksgiving today is like this feast. Today, people in many countries have feasts to celebrate good harvests.

The American Indians got meat from hunting. In the forest were deer, bears, rabbits, and squirrels. In the very early days, there were buffalo.

After a while, settlers began to arrive. They came from the east. The settlers wanted the land. The American Indians would not give up the land. Because of this, there were many, many wars. The settlers finally won. They forced the American Indians out. Most of one group, the Cherokees, moved west. Some still live in the mountains of North Carolina. Another group, the Tuscaroras, went to New York. They still live there. But life was never the same again for the American Indians.

REVIEW

CHECK YOUR FACTS

1. Who first lived where Burlington is today?
2. Each American Indian village had (one big farm/many small farms).
3. In what two ways did the American Indians get food?
4. What did the American Indians do in the fall to celebrate the harvest?
5. What did the settlers and the American Indians fight over?

THINK ABOUT IT

Did any American Indian groups ever live in your area? What were their names?

Lesson 3: Early Settlers

The first settlers started coming to the land that is now Burlington about 1733. That was about 250 years ago.

In those days, the whole family worked very hard. Most people were farmers. The family members plowed and planted. They raised and killed hogs. The women also had to cook and sew and knit. They made most of the clothes.

Making a wool dress or a pair of pants was a hard job. The men cut the wool from the sheep. Then, the women washed it, dried it, and spun it into thread. They wove the thread into cloth. Then, they dyed the cloth with bark or herbs. They made buttons out of wood or from the horn of an animal.

Settlers cut down trees to build log cabins.

The settlers helped each other in many ways. Sometimes, they would get together to help one family build a barn. After the work was done, there would be wrestling, jumping contests, and shooting matches. Some people liked to pitch horseshoes. They also played a game like baseball! Only it was called "rounders" then.

Sometimes, the farmers went hunting. This helped put more meat on the table. There were wild turkeys, quail, and pigeons. There were also beavers, rabbits, and squirrels.

Religion was important to the early settlers. Many people moved to the Burlington area so they could pray as they wanted. They did not have churches at first. They went to camp meetings. People would come from many miles away. They camped in their wagons. Most meetings lasted 2 or 3 days. Some meetings lasted a week.

REVIEW

CHECK YOUR FACTS

1. When did the first settlers come to Burlington?
2. What kind of work did most early settlers do?
3. The settlers (did/did not) help each other.
4. At first, the settlers (did/did not) have churches.

THINK ABOUT IT

Compare the way you live with the way thc early settlers lived. Talk about your parents' jobs. Describe how your family gets food and clothing. Discuss what your family does together and with friends. How is what you do different from what the settlers did?

Lesson 4: Burlington Gets Its Name

The first settlers arrived in the Burlington area long before it got its name.

Edwin Holt built the first cotton mill about 1837. That was important. It brought jobs to the area. Seventeen years later, the North Carolina Railroad Company decided to build its repair shops there. The community became known as Company Shops because of this. The community grew. A hotel for railroad passengers was built. The telegraph came, too. That was important because it brought news to Company Shops.

Then, in 1886, the railroad company moved the repair shops to another state. Many people thought everyone would leave the community. But the community refused to die. After all, it had the cotton mills, the hotels, and even a coffin factory.

Some community leaders got together. They said that the community needed a new name. They chose the name *Burlington*. A newspaper was started. The little town made up a motto: "I'll tell the world." That showed the spirit of the people of Burlington.

After that, the people built roads in place of the muddy trails. They started dairy farms. The cotton mills grew, and more were built. The coffin company grew, too. It even made coffins for people's pets.

Other people in North Carolina were surprised that Burlington lived through such bad

This is an old picture of Burlington.

times. One of the newspapers talked about Burlington. It said, "No town in the state has shown its ability to come back better than Burlington." This made the people who lived in Burlington very proud of their community.

REVIEW

CHECK YOUR FACTS

1. The first settlers arrived (before/after) Burlington got its name.
2. Why was the first cotton mill important?
3. What was Burlington's first name?
4. What happened to the railroad repair shops in 1886?
5. Who chose Burlington's name?

THINK ABOUT IT

How did your community get its name?

Lesson 5: Burlington's Factories

NEW WORDS

factory

textile

Everywhere in Burlington today, people are working. Some work in stores, hospitals, restaurants, and schools. Others may fix cars, bicycles, or television sets. Many others work in **factories.** These are buildings in which things are made.

There are many factories in Burlington. Some make foods, such as sandwich spreads and whipped cream. Others make bricks, furniture, and boxes. Most factories in Burlington make **textiles,** or woven cloth.

In textile factories, workers make thread and weave cloth. Then they use the threads and cloth to make clothes. They also make carpets, drapes, blankets, sheets, and furniture coverings. Most of these textiles are sold outside Burlington. In this way, the people of Burlington earn money. They use money to buy food, machines, and other things. Many of these things are not grown or

This is one of the factories in Burlington.

Women work in an early textile factory.

made in Burlington. The people use money to buy or rent homes. They use it to pay doctors, teachers, and other workers.

The largest textile company in Burlington is Burlington Industries. Use your time line to find the year when it was started. Then, its factory had 200 workers. Today, Burlington Industries has thousands of workers in many factories all over the world.

REVIEW

CHECK YOUR FACTS

1. What is done in a factory?
2. What is a textile?
3. How do many people in Burlington earn money to pay for things they need?
4. What is the largest textile company in Burlington?
5. Burlington Industries has (one factory/many factories).

THINK ABOUT IT

Are there any factories in your community? If so, what do they make?

Lesson 6: Burlington's Resources

NEW WORDS

natural resource

Why are there so many textile factories in Burlington? Part of the answer is Burlington's natural resources. A **natural resource** is something found on or in the earth that people can use. Soil, trees, water, and oil are a few of many natural resources.

Burlington is near land that is good for growing cotton. It has a good water supply. Long ago, textile factories used water power to run their machines. Today, water is still used in the dyes that give color to the textiles.

Burlington has other resources, too. These are not natural resources. But they are important in making textiles. People who work are a resource. Factories could not run without people.

Burlington has buildings for the factories. There are tools and machines for the workers to use. These are all resources. There are many ways for people and things to get in and out of

Cloth is made from the fluffy part of the cotton plant.

This woman works in a modern textile factory.

Burlington. Airplanes, trains, trucks, and cars are used. These are resources, too. So are schools, hospitals, and libraries. These help people and serve their needs.

REVIEW

CHECK YOUR FACTS

1. What is a natural resource?
2. Today, the machines in textile factories (are/are not) run with water power.
3. People (are/are not) a resource of the community.
4. What resources are found in factories?
5. How do people and things get in and out of Burlington?

THINK ABOUT IT

Name some resources in your community. Tell how each is used.

CHAPTER REVIEW

WATCH YOUR WORDS

1. ___ is the story of the past.
   Time line History
   Revolution
2. The ___ is the time crops are gathered.
   harvest industry resource
3. A(n) ___ is a building in which things are made.
   harvest industry factory
4. A ___ is something found on or in the earth that people can use.
   natural resource factory
   history

CHECK YOUR FACTS

5. All people and places (do/do not) have a history.
6. What does a time line show?
7. What people were the first to live in the Burlington area?
8. What happened to most of the Cherokees?
9. In the early days in Burlington, the whole family (did/did not) work.
10. The first settlers came to Burlington (before/after) it got its name.
11. Why was Burlington first called Company Shops?
12. Name two things the factories in Burlington make.
13. Name two natural resources.
14. Above all, what do factories need to run?

THINK ABOUT IT

15. Why do you think we study history?
16. Was the coming of the settlers good or bad for the American Indians? Give reasons for your answer.
17. Today, many of the things we use are made in factories. How do you think the early settlers filled most of their needs?
18. Which do you think are most important, natural resources or "people" resources? Give reasons for your answer.
19. In what ways does Burlington seem like your community? In what ways is it different?
20. List all the ways you can think of in which communities are different from one another.
21. You have learned that history is the story of the past. List some ways in which this story can be told.

CHAPTER 5 OUR NATION'S CAPITAL

Lesson 1: Building a New City

Washington, DC, is another important city in the Eastern United States. It is our nation's capital. Our nation's government is located there. *DC* stands for "District of Columbia." This means that our nation's capital is not located in any state. It is in a special area. This area is called the District of Columbia.

The United States was founded over 200 years ago. The first President was George Washington. Washington became President in 1789. At that time, our nation did not really have a capital city. For a while, the government was in New

York City. Then it was moved to Philadelphia. But the nation needed a city specially built to be the capital.

In 1790, government leaders decided to locate the capital city in the middle of the United States. Look at the map of the Eastern United States on page 44. Most of this area is made up of the 13 states that started our nation. Find Washington, DC. Remember, in 1790, travel was hard and slow. People rode horses or rode in wagons pulled by horses. They did not have cars, planes, trains, or motorboats. So people wanted the capital in the middle of the nation. That way, it would be easier to travel there.

George Washington picked the place. It is on the Potomac River between the states of Virginia and Maryland. Andrew Ellicott and Benjamin Banneker laid out the borders of the district. Pierre L'Enfant drew up a plan for the city. The capital was named for President Washington.

REVIEW

CHECK YOUR FACTS

1. Washington, DC, (is/is not) located in a state.
2. In 1789, the United States (did/did not) have a special capital city.
3. Where did government leaders decide to locate the capital city in 1790?
4. When our nation was new, it was (hard/easy) to travel.
5. Who drew up the plan for the new capital?

THINK ABOUT IT

Why is Washington, DC, no longer located in the middle of the United States?

WHERE WE ARE IN TIME AND PLACE

TIME LINE FOR WASHINGTON

1776	1789	1800	1814
American independence declared	American government established	Government moves to Washington, the new capital	British troops attack Washington

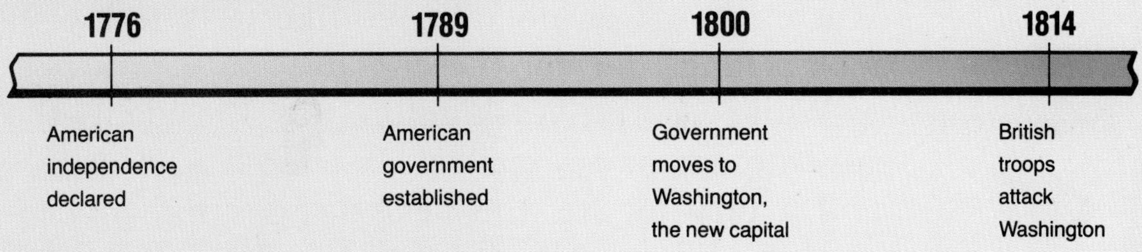

WASHINGTON, DC

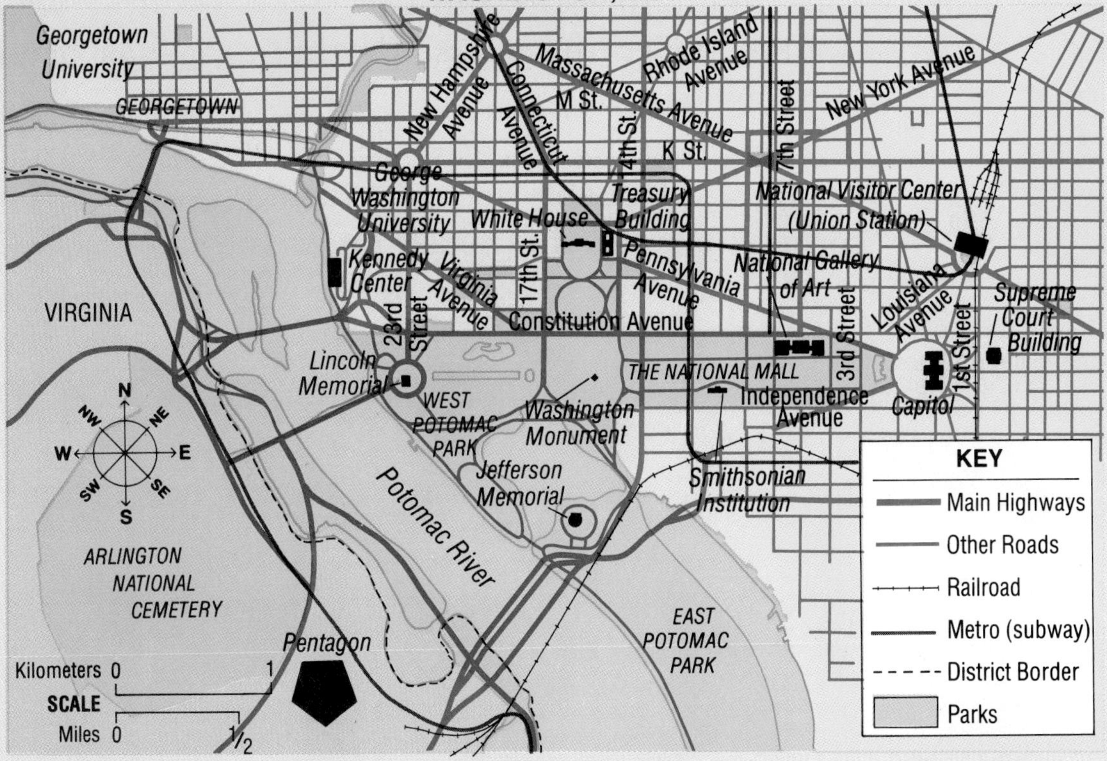

Lesson 2: Washington Grows

NEW WORDS

- Capitol
- monument

Today, Washington, DC, is a big city. But Washington was not always like it is today. It took a long time for the city to grow.

While George Washington was President, the government had a contest. It offered $500 prizes and a city lot for the best designs for government buildings. The **Capitol** was to be the main government building in Washington. The prize for the capitol building was won by Dr. William Thornton. The building Thornton designed was much like the Capitol today. But it was smaller. Over the years, the building has been made bigger.

The prize for the President's house was won by James Hoban. George Washington laid the cornerstone for the house on October 13, 1797.

This painting shows the Capitol in 1824.

The President's house was not known as the White House then. It was called the President's house or the President's palace.

In the year 1800, the government moved to the new capital city. John Adams, the second President, was in office then. He was the first President to live in the President's house. He moved into the house in November 1800. But the house was not yet finished. Very little of the city was built up.

In the many years since then, Washington has grown. At different times, government leaders have had new buildings and monuments built. A **monument** helps people remember a person or an event. Today, there are many important buildings and monuments in Washington. They tell much about our nation's history.

REVIEW

CHECK YOUR FACTS

1. Washington (was/was not) always a big city with many buildings and monuments.
2. The President's house (was/was not) always known as the White House.
3. When did the government move to the new capital city?
4. Who was the first President to live in the President's house?
5. What does a monument help people do?

THINK ABOUT IT

Are there any government buildings in your community? What are they?

Lesson 3: A Tour of Washington

NEW WORDS

- **Congress**
- **Senate**
- **House of Representatives**
- **President**
- **Supreme Court**

Someday, you might take a trip to Washington. You can learn much about the United States by visiting its capital. You could take a bus tour of Washington. Here are things you could see.

At the top of page 67 is our nation's Capitol. The Capitol is the building where Congress meets. **Congress** makes laws for the United States as a whole. It is made up of two groups of men and women. One group is called the **Senate.** The other is called the **House of Representatives.**

Below is the White House. It is where our President lives today. The **President** is the leader of the United States. The President sees that the laws of our nation are followed.

The White House is the President's home.

Top: This is the Capitol today. The tall building at the far left is the Washington Monument. *Left*: This is the Supreme Court Building.

At the bottom of page 67 is the Supreme Court Building. The Supreme Court meets here. The **Supreme Court** is the highest court in the United States. The judges of the Supreme Court are called justices. They decide whether the nation's laws are being obeyed or broken.

The Washington Monument honors George Washington. Remember, he was our first President. He helped our nation get started.

There are other sights you could see in the Washington area. You could go to Arlington National Cemetery in Virginia. The Tomb of the Unknown Soldier is there. This monument honors soldiers who died fighting for their country. A few soldiers whose names are not known are buried there.

REVIEW

WATCH YOUR WORDS

1. The ___ makes laws for the United States as a whole.
Supreme Court   President
Congress

2. Congress is made up of the ___ and the House of Representatives.
Senate   President
Supreme Court

3. The ___ is the leader of the United States.
Supreme Court   President
House of Representatives

CHECK YOUR FACTS

4. Who was the first President of the United States?

5. Where is the Tomb of the Unknown Soldier?

THINK ABOUT IT

Which of the buildings and monuments in Washington would you most like to see? Why?

Lesson 4: How Our Government Works

The United States was founded over 200 years ago. In those days, kings and queens ruled most nations on Earth. People did not choose their

NEW WORDS

- **elect**
- **Constitution**
- **legislative branch**
- **senator**
- **represen-tative**
- **executive branch**
- **judicial branch**
- **Bill of Rights**

George Washington was the first President of the United States.

leaders. People had little to say about how they were ruled. Kings and queens could sometimes do anything they pleased. It did not matter whether most people liked what they did or not.

The United States was different. It had a new kind of government. The government was new for two reasons. First, government leaders were **elected,** or chosen by voters. Second, the leaders could not do anything they pleased. There were laws that said how the government was to be run. The laws said what the government could and could not do.

The highest laws in the United States are set down in the **Constitution** (KON stuh TOO shun). The Constitution was written by our nation's leaders almost 200 years ago. It was approved by the people of the first 13 states. The government that the United States has today is based on the Constitution. Here is a description of how our government works.

The government of the United States has three branches, or parts. Each has some power, but not all the power. This was done so that no one branch could get too powerful. With too much power, one branch could take away people's rights.

The first part of our government is called the **legislative** (LEJ iss LAY tiv) **branch.** Congress is the legislative branch of the nation. Congress makes the laws for the United States as a whole. It is made up of two houses, or parts. The Senate is one house. It has 100 members. They are called **senators.** There are two senators from each state. The other part of Congress is the House of Representatives. It has 435 members. They are called **representatives.** The more people a state has, the more representatives it has. Each state has at least one representative. Congress makes laws. It does not carry out the laws. Laws must be agreed to by both houses of Congress. Then they go to the President for approval.

The second part of our government is called the **executive** (eg ZEK yuh tiv) **branch.** The President is head of the executive branch. The President carries out the laws of the nation. The executive branch sees to it that people do what the law says. The President is also the head of the armed forces of the United States.

The third part of our government is called the **judicial** (joo DISH ul) **branch.** It is made up of the Supreme Court and other courts. The courts tell

Each court is run by a judge.

when the law is being obeyed or not. They say whether or not laws passed by Congress follow the Constitution.

All three branches of our government follow the laws of the United States. They respect the rights of the people and of the states. Part of the Constitution says what the rights of the people are. This part of the Constitution is called the **Bill of Rights.** The Constitution also says which powers belong to the national government. It says which powers remain with the states.

REVIEW

WATCH YOUR WORDS

1. The ___ is headed by the President.
executive branch
judicial branch   Congress

2. The ___ includes the Supreme Court.
executive branch
judicial branch   Congress

3. Members of Congress are called senators and___.
constitutions   elections
representatives

4. The government of the United States is based on the ___.
Constitution   Congress
judicial branch

5. In the United States, most government leaders are___.
constituted   elected
senators

CHECK YOUR FACTS

6. How were most nations ruled when the United States was founded?

7. How was the government of the United States new and different?

8. What is the Constitution?

9. Name the three branches of the government.

10. The Constitution (does/does not) say what the rights of the people are.

THINK ABOUT IT

Some nations are still ruled by kings or queens. Name one.

CHAPTER REVIEW

WATCH YOUR WORDS

1. Washington has many important buildings and___.
   monuments capitols districts
2. Congress meets in the___.
   Supreme Court Capitol
   executive branch
3. The judges of the ___ decide whether laws are being obeyed or broken.
   Supreme Court Senate
   legislative branch
4. Congress is the ___ of our nation's government.
   judicial branch
   executive branch
   legislative branch
5. In Congress, each state has two___.
   judges candidates senators
6. The ___ is part of the Constitution of the United States.
   Bill of Rights political party
   district
7. Courts are included in the___.
   judicial branch
   legislative branch
   executive branch

CHECK YOUR FACTS

8. Where is the center of our nation's government located?
9. What was the White House called at first?
10. What are the names of the two parts of Congress?
11. How many branches of government are there?
12. What does the Bill of Rights say?

TRY SOMETHING NEW

13. Find out the name of the capital city of your state.
14. Draw a picture of one of the buildings or monuments in Washington.
15. Suppose a friend from another state was visiting you. List some buildings in your community that you would like to show your friend.
16. Make a chart that shows the three branches of government and their parts.

UNIT REVIEW

WATCH YOUR WORDS

areas	continents	key	North Pole	President
capital	directions	map	occupations	South Pole
Capitol	globe	monuments	oceans	states
cardinal	government	mountain	photograph	symbols
communities	grid	range	populations	urban areas

A(n)___ is a model of Earth. On Earth, there are large areas of land called ___ . There are also large bodies of water called ___ . North and south are ___ . The ___ is at the "top" of a globe. At the "bottom" is the ___ . East and west are the other two ___ directions.

People get the things they need and want in ___ . Cities have large ___ , or numbers of people. They also have large land ___ . The people in cities have many different ___ , or ways to make a living. Cities and their suburbs make up ___ .

An aerial ___ can show you much about a community. However, a(n) ___ is better. It is a drawing of Earth or part of Earth. Mapmakers use little pictures called ___ to show you where things are. You can find out what these mean in the map ___ . Mapmakers help you find places by putting squares on the map. These squares form a(n) ___ .

A nation has its own land, people, and ___ . Our nation is made up of 50 ___ . Governments are located in ___ cities. The Eastern United States lies between the Atlantic Ocean and a(n) ___ called the Appalachians.

Washington, our nation's capital, has many important buildings and ___ . Congress meets in a building called the ___ . The ___ lives in the White House.

CHECK YOUR FACTS

1. Name the four oceans.

2. Name the cardinal directions.

3. What does a community always have?

4. A city has a (large/small) area.

5. What are the two things that make up an urban area?

6. Give reasons people live in communities.

7. What do police officers do in a community?

8. How can you find out what the symbols on a map mean?

9. How can you help people find places on a map?

10. On what continent is the United States located?

11. All people and places (do/do not) have a history.
12. In what two ways did the American Indians get their food?
13. The early settlers (did/did not) usually help each other.
14. The first settlers arrived (before/after) Burlington got its name.
15. What do most factories in Burlington make?
16. Water (is/is not) one of our natural resources.
17. What does DC stand for?
18. How did the city of Washington get its name?
19. What are the two parts of Congress?

CLOSE THE MAP GAP

20. Draw a globe. Show and label the North Pole and the South Pole. Do the same for North America, South America, the Atlantic Ocean, and the Pacific Ocean.
21. Draw a map of your classroom. Use symbols for important things. Explain the symbols in a key.

USE YOUR GLOBES

22. Look at the globes on page 16. What ocean is west of South America?
23. Look at the globes again. What continent is farther south than any other?
24. Look at the globe on page 19. What two nations border the United States?
25. Look at the globe on page 21. Suppose you were at the middle of Earth looking toward the North Pole. What direction would be on your right?
26. Look at the globe on page 19. Name the three capital cities shown.

THINK ABOUT IT

27. The prefix *ant* means "opposite." What is Antarctica the opposite of?
28. Suppose you wanted to find your way around a new community. Would you rather have a map or a globe? Why?
29. Today, the United States is much larger than it was in 1790. Should the capital be moved from Washington to the new "middle" of the nation? Why, or why not?

TRY SOMETHING NEW

30. Get a map of your area. Find the place where you live.
31. Write a letter to a government leader about a problem you are concerned about.

THE MIDDLE UNITED STATES

UNIT 2

CHAPTER 1 LEARNING FROM MAPS

Lesson 1: Mapping the Middle United States

NEW WORDS

- plain
- river
- boundary
- lake

In this unit, you will study a lot about Kansas City and Houston (HYOO stun). These are cities in the middle part of the United States. This area is very large. It lies between two groups of mountains. The Appalachian Mountains are in the east. The Rocky Mountains are in the west.

The land between these mountains is mostly flat. Areas of flat land are called **plains.** The middle part of our nation has two large areas of plains. They are divided by the Missouri (mi ZUR ee) River. East of the river are the Central Plains.

West of the river are the Great Plains. Much of these plains is rich farmland. A lot of the nation's food is grown in the Middle United States.

Rivers are very important to the Middle United States. **Rivers** carry water that has fallen to Earth as snow or rain. They usually start in the mountains and flow toward the sea. The most important river in the Middle United States is the Mississippi (MISS i SIP ee) River.

The map on the next page shows the Middle United States. There are many symbols on the map. Find the special lines that show rivers. Now find the lines that divide the states. State lines are one kind of border. Borders are also called **boundaries.** Another kind of border divides nations. It looks like this **---** . Sometimes rivers are borders between states or nations. Where this is so, mapmakers do not draw a border. They let the river be the border.

Between the United States and Canada you see five large lakes. **Lakes** are large bodies of water surrounded by land. These five lakes are called the Great Lakes. They are the largest group of lakes in the world. Like rivers, the Great Lakes are important for travel and for shipping.

Cities are also shown on the map. The large dots stand for cities. Find Kansas City, Missouri. Then find some other cities.

Kansas City, Missouri, lies almost in the center of the United States. As you will see, this location has been very important to Kansas City.

THE MIDDLE UNITED STATES
CANADA
NORTH DAKOTA
Bismarck
MINNESOTA
St. Paul
Minneapolis
Lake Superior
Lake Huron
Lake Michigan
WISCONSIN
SOUTH DAKOTA
Pierre
Madison
MICHIGAN
Detroit
Lansing
Lake Erie
UNITED STATES
IOWA
Chicago
OHIO
Missouri River
NEBRASKA
Des Moines
ILLINOIS
INDIANA
Columbus
Lincoln
Kansas City
Springfield
Indianapolis
Ohio River
Kansas River
Frankfort
Jefferson City
KANSAS
Topeka
Kansas City
KENTUCKY
MISSOURI
ROCKY MOUNTAINS
Nashville
APPALACHIAN MOUNTAINS
OKLAHOMA
TENNESSEE
ARKANSAS
Mississippi River
Oklahoma City
Little Rock
ALABAMA
N
NW
NE
W
E
SW
SE
S
TEXAS
Jackson
Montgomery
MISSISSIPPI
Baton Rouge
Austin
LOUISIANA
Houston
KEY
Mountains
State Borders
State Capitals
Country Borders
Cities
MEXICO

REVIEW

WATCH YOUR WORDS

1. A___is the same as a border.
   plain boundary range
2. A___is an area of flat land.
   plain boundary lake

CHECK YOUR FACTS

3. What groups of mountains border the Middle United States?
4. What river is most important to the Middle United States?
5. What large bodies of water lie between the United States and Canada?

THINK ABOUT IT

Why is land that is flat good for farming?

Lesson 2: Using a Compass

NEW WORD
compass

Maps can show you directions. To find north, south, east, and west, you use a compass. A **compass** on a map is a drawing with arrows. The arrows point in each direction. This drawing shows a compass.

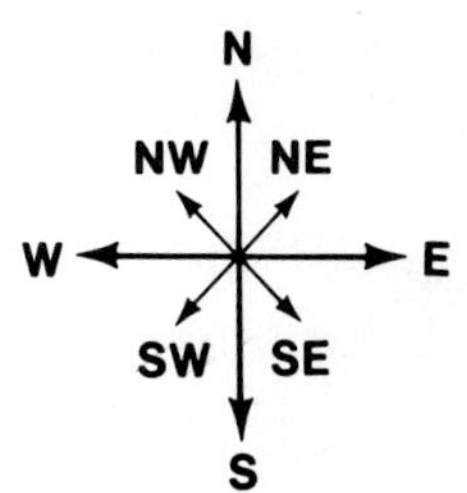

Now find the compass on the map on the facing page. Find the letters on the compass. You know some of the directions the letters stand for. Find the *N*. *N* stands for north. What direction does *S* stand for? What do *W* and *E* stand for? There are other letters on the compass, too.

Pretend you are in Kansas City, Missouri. You want to visit Chicago, Illinois. Chicago is north of Kansas City. Chicago is also east of Kansas City.

The direction to Chicago is between the arrow pointing north and the arrow pointing east. It is

FUN FACTS

The word *compass* has another meaning. A compass also is a useful tool for finding your way. Have you ever picked up things with a magnet? A compass works like a magnet. The North Pole and South Pole of Earth are magnetic. A compass is a magnet that can turn in a circle. You take the compass out and hold it level. It will always point north and south. Now you know these directions. Then you can figure out which way is east and which way is west.

The compass was invented long ago by the Chinese. They floated some straw in a bowl of water. They put a piece of iron on it to make a compass. Later, sailors from Arabia and Europe made the compass better. Now you can buy a small compass that will fit in your pocket.

between north and east. We say that Chicago is northeast of Kansas City. *NE* stands for northeast. What do *NW, SW,* and *SE* stand for?

Now find Houston in southeastern Texas. To travel to Austin, you go northwest. To travel to Baton Rouge (BAT in ROOZH), Louisiana, you go northeast.

REVIEW

CHECK YOUR FACTS

Look at the Map

1. Suppose you are in Jackson, Mississippi. What direction is Little Rock, Arkansas?
2. Suppose you are in Springfield, Illinois. What direction is Indianapolis, Indiana?
3. What state borders South Dakota on the south?

Look at the Lesson

4. You (can/cannot) tell directions from a map.
5. What is a compass?

THINK ABOUT IT

What do you think the directions *WSW* and *NNE* stand for?

Lesson 3: Using a Distance Scale

NEW WORDS

distance

distance scale

How far is it from your desk to your teacher's desk? If you don't know, you could use a ruler. Your desk is not very far from your teacher's desk.

It would be harder to measure how far your community is from another community. It would take too long and could cost a lot of money. There is a better way.

You can use a map to find the distance between places. **Distance** is how far one place is from another. You can measure the distance between places on a map with a distance scale. A **distance scale** shows what a distance on the map equals in real distance. This real distance is usually in kilometers or miles. Below, you can see what a distance scale looks like.

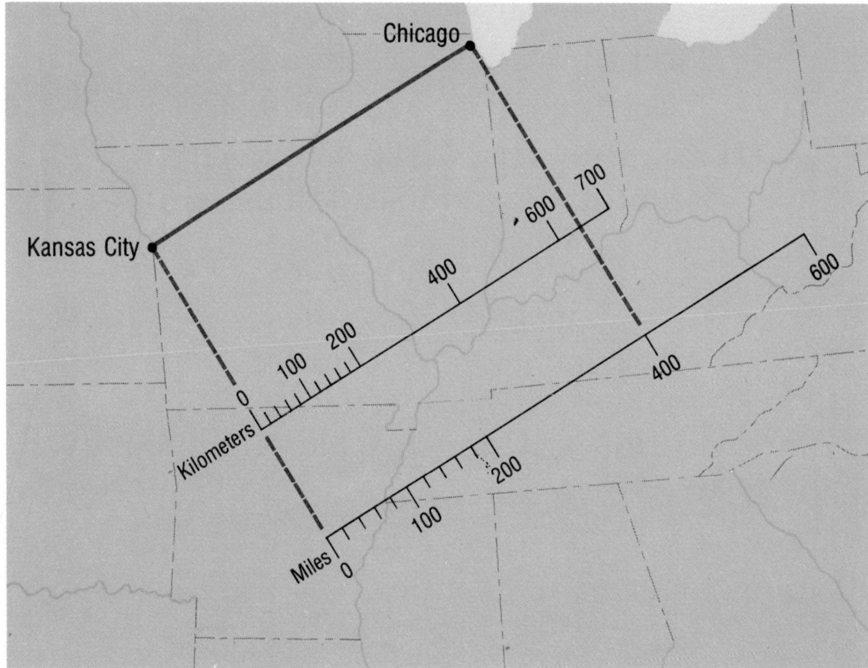

Suppose you want to find out how far it is from Kansas City to Chicago. First, find Kansas City and Chicago on the map. Then use a ruler to measure the distance between them on the map. You should get a distance of 5 centimeters, or 2 inches.

Look at the scale for the map on page 85. It says that 1 centimeter on this map equals 128 kilometers on Earth. It also says that 1 inch on this map equals 200 miles on Earth. Thus, 5 centimeters on the map equals 640 kilometers in real distance. Also, 2 inches on the map equals 400 miles in real distance.

How do you know? You add. Add 128 kilometers for every centimeter you measured. Or, add 200 miles for every inch you measured. That gives you the real distance between Chicago and Kansas City.

1 centimeter = 128 kilometers
1 centimeter = 128 kilometers
1 centimeter = 128 kilometers
1 centimeter = 128 kilometers
1 centimeter = 128 kilometers
---
5 centimeters = 640 kilometers

1 inch = 200 miles
1 inch = 200 miles
---
2 inches = 400 miles

You will find a distance scale on almost every map. Maps show different areas. So scales are of different sizes. On some maps, 1 inch may equal 50 miles or even 1000 miles.

THE MIDDLE UNITED STATES

Look at the map again. It shows many large cities in the United States. Use the distance scale to find how far Oklahoma City, Oklahoma is from Pierre, South Dakota. How many kilometers is it? Is the distance smaller or larger than the distance between Springfield, Illinois, and Lincoln, Nebraska?

Now find the distance from Little Rock, Arkansas, to Montgomery, Alabama. Is the distance almost the same as the distance from Chicago to Kansas City? What is the distance from Austin, Texas, to Nashville, Tennessee?

Now play a game with a classmate. Call out two cities. Have your classmate measure the distance between them. You do the same. Then compare your answers. Now have your classmate pick out the cities. Again, both of you measure the distance and compare answers.

REVIEW

CHECK YOUR FACTS

Look at the Maps

1. About how many kilometers or miles is it from Kansas City, Missouri, to Jefferson City, Missouri?

2. About how many kilometers or miles is it from Chicago, Illinois, to Bismarck, North Dakota?

Look at the Lesson

3. How can distance be measured on a map?
4. What units of real distance are usually shown on a map?

TRY SOMETHING NEW

Make a map that has a distance scale. It can be a map of your schoolroom, home, or neighborhood.

CHAPTER REVIEW

WATCH YOUR WORDS

1. ___ carry rainwater toward the sea.
   Lakes Rivers Plains
2. ___ are large bodies of water surrounded by land.
   Lakes Rivers Boundaries
3. A ___ has arrows pointing in each direction.
   compass distance scale boundary
4. A ___ helps you find how far one place is from another.
   compass distance scale plain
5. A___is an area of flat land.
   compass distance plain

CHECK YOUR FACTS

6. In what area of the United States is Kansas City, Missouri located?
7. Farming (is/is not) important on the Central Plains and Great Plains.
8. What is the largest group of lakes in the world?
9. How do you find directions on a map?
10. What does *SE* stand for?
11. How do you find distance on a map?
12. What should you use to measure the actual distance on a map?
13. Ten kilometers (is/is not) equal to ten miles.
14. On a map, what does 1 centimeter = 128 kilometers mean?

Use Your Map

15. Look at the map on page 85. How many states border on Missouri?
16. What two nations border on the Middle United States?
17. What is the capital of Kansas?
18. Suppose you were in Des Moines (duh MOIN), Iowa. In what direction would you have to travel to get to St. Paul, Minnesota?
19. About how far is Columbus, Ohio, from Lansing, Michigan?

THINK ABOUT IT

20. Why do rivers usually start in the mountains and flow to the sea?
21. What other kind of compass is there besides the kind on maps?
22. Natural borders are things like rivers, lakes, oceans, and mountains. The borders between states or nations often follow such natural borders. Why?

CHAPTER 2 LEARNING ABOUT KANSAS CITY

Lesson 1: Trading-post Days

NEW WORDS

wagon train

warehouse

Long ago, American Indians lived where Kansas City is now. The Osage (oh SAYJ) and Kansas peoples hunted in the forests. They fished in the Missouri and the Kansas rivers. There were also a few explorers and fur trappers in the area.

In 1821, a trading post was started where the Kansas River and Missouri River meet. The people who started the post traded with the American Indians and trappers. The traders wanted animal furs. The American Indians and trappers wanted clothes, food, and tools.

WHERE WE ARE IN TIME AND PLACE

TIME LINE FOR KANSAS CITY

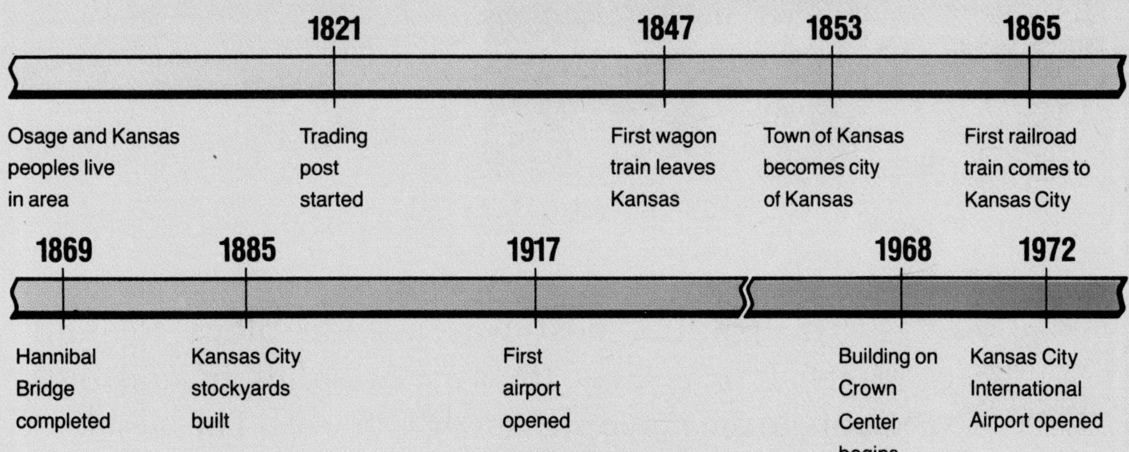

TRAILS TO THE WEST-1850

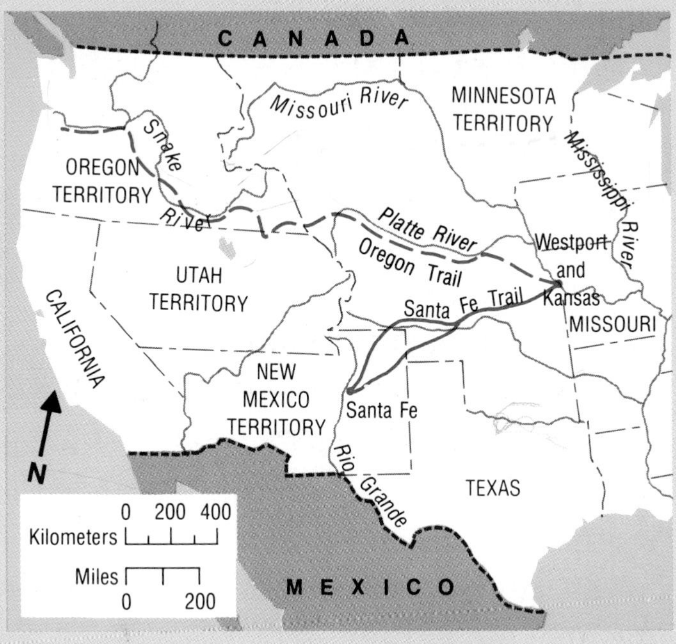

Kansas City's location is important to its history. It began in 1821 as a trading post where the Missouri and Kansas rivers meet. Beginning in 1847, wagon trains started west from Kansas City. A railroad connected Kansas City to the East in 1865. In 1869, the Hannibal Bridge across the Missouri let trains go west from Kansas City. In 1917, the first airport opened. Kansas City became an important stopping place for planes crossing the country.

Kansas City was once a small town.

The trading post was a good place to land boats. It was easy to bring supplies in and out. Soon, other people settled there. The settlers sold supplies to American Indians, trappers, and people going west.

The trading post was growing. Other posts opened nearby. One trading post was called Westport. The other was called Kansas. These trading posts soon became little towns.

After 1840, there was not much fur trading. But people were still moving west. Many traveled in wagons. A group of wagons was called a **wagon train.** These trains started near Westport and Kansas. The first wagon train left in 1847.

Business was good in Westport and Kansas. So the two towns grew. The people built stores, hotels, and warehouses. A **warehouse** is a building in which things are stored.

The town of Kansas became the city of Kansas in 1853. It did not look like much of a city. The buildings were made of wood. They were small and plain. But Kansas City was in a good place to grow.

REVIEW

CHECK YOUR FACTS

Look at the Time Line

1. Which came first, the wagon trains or the railroad trains?
2. How many years were there between the first airport and the newest one?

Look at the Lesson

3. Where was the trading post started in 1821?
4. What were the two nearby trading posts called?
5. What happened to the town of Kansas in 1853?

THINK ABOUT IT

Kansas City grew up near where two rivers meet. Is there a body of water near your community? How is it important?

Lesson 2: Kansas City Grows

NEW WORD

stockyards

The first railroad came to Kansas City in 1865. Then the river town began to grow into a big city. The railroad brought more people. It connected Kansas City with cities in the East. It carried mail and supplies back and forth quickly.

In 1869, the Hannibal Bridge was built. It was the first railroad bridge across the Missouri River. This meant that railroad trains could go farther west. They did not have to stop at the river. One year latcr, eight different railroads connected Kansas City with other places.

In the years that followed, Kansas City became a marketplace for wheat. The wheat was grown on farms in the area. Railroads began bringing cattle from the West. Kansas City became a center for the cattle trade. In 1885, the Kansas City stockyards were built. These **stockyards** were like huge pens. They held the cattle that were going to market. At this time, flour mills and meat-packing plants were started. These industries are still important to Kansas City.

During these years, people tried to make Kansas City a nice place to live. The newspaper ran stories about what the city needed. One story said, "Kansas City needs good streets and better street lights. It needs fire fighters and a better police force." The people built a city hall, a public library, and an opera house. They built parks and planted trees along the streets.

In 1917, Kansas City's first airport opened. It was just a landing place in a grassy field. Many

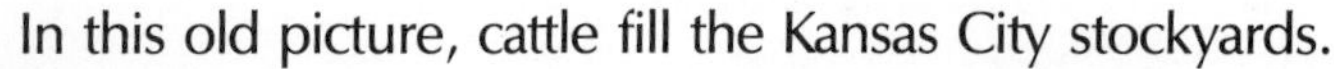

In this old picture, cattle fill the Kansas City stockyards.

airline companies came to Kansas City over the years. In 1972, an international airport was opened. This meant that planes could fly from Kansas City to other countries.

Rivers, railroads, and airports are important to Kansas City. The location of Kansas City is important, too. Because of these things, Kansas City grew. It became a place where many goods are sold. It became a center for business, shipping, and transportation. It became a big city. Then, in recent years, Kansas City began to get smaller. Businesses moved to the suburbs around the city. As a result, some of the people moved away.

The leaders of the city drew up a plan. They wanted to stop the city from getting much smaller. They wanted to make the best use of the city's land. They wanted to choose the best places to build new houses and businesses. All these things were part of their plan.

REVIEW

CHECK YOUR FACTS

1. When did the first railroad come to Kansas City?
2. What river did the Hannibal Bridge cross?
3. Flour milling and meat packing (are/are not) still important in Kansas City.
4. In what year were the Kansas City stockyards built?
5. When did the first Kansas City airport open?
6. The location of Kansas City (was/was not) important in its growth.

THINK ABOUT IT

How are the wheat and cattle trades related to flour milling and meat packing?

Lesson 3: Land Use in Kansas City

NEW WORDS

- land-use map
- residential land
- commercial land
- industrial land
- public land
- vacant land
- transportation land

In a home, there are special places for all the things the family does. In the same way, people use the land in cities for different things. We can show how people use land in cities with a special map. It is called a **land-use map.**

On page 95 is a land-use map of the Kansas City area. The colors show you how the land is used. Look at the key. To read the key, you will need to learn some special words.

Land on which people live is called **residential** (REZ uh DEN chul) **land.** Suppose you visit the parts of a city where people live. There you will find homes and apartment houses. Residential land is colored gold on the map.

Land where people have built stores, movies, and office buildings is called **commercial** (kuh MUR shul) **land.** If you visit commercial land, you will find mostly stores and offices. You will not find many places for people to live. Commercial land is colored black on the map. Where is the commercial land in Kansas City, Missouri? Is it spread out? Is most of it in the same place?

Land where people make things is called **industrial** (in DUS tree ul) **land.** Suppose you visit industrial land. There you will find factories and other places where people make things. There is another color for industrial land. It is purple.

There are three more colors on your map. One is green. This stands for **public land.** This is

LAND USE IN KANSAS CITY AREA

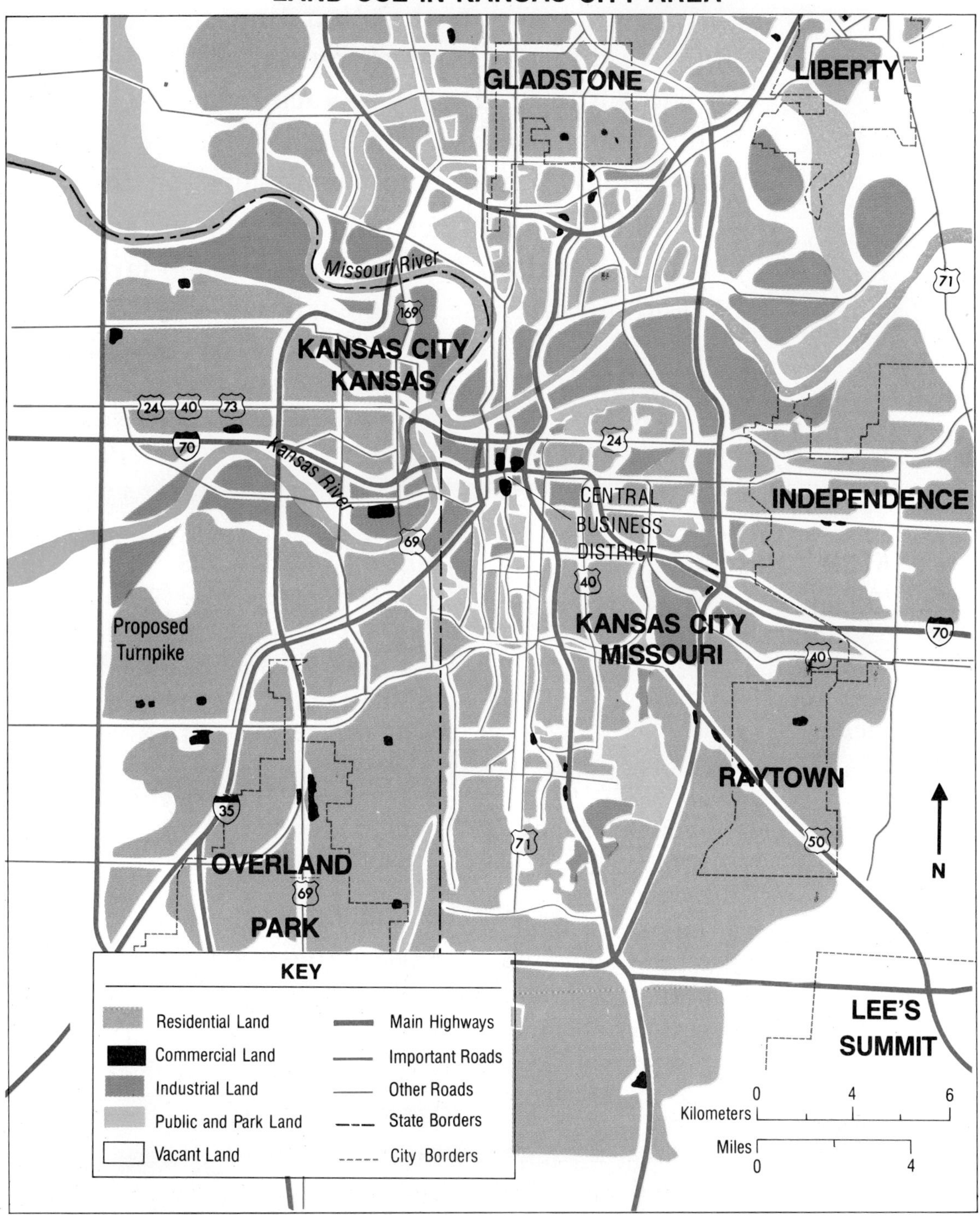

land owned by all the people in Kansas City. Here you find schools and hospitals. You find playgrounds and parks. You find museums and libraries and government buildings.

The white in the key is **vacant land.** This land is not being used yet. It might be empty lots or grassy fields. Find some vacant land on the map.

Find some red lines on your map. These stand for **transportation** (TRANS por TAY shun) **land.** This is land people use to go from place to place. Land used for roads, railroads, train stations, and airports is transportation land.

REVIEW

WATCH YOUR WORDS

1. Land with stores and office buildings on it is ___.
residential land
commercial land
industrial land

2. Land with factories on it is ___.
public land industrial land
commercial land

3. ___ is owned by the people.
Public land Industrial land
Vacant land

4. People live on ___.
public land residential land
vacant land

5. People use ___ to go from place to place.
residential land vacant land
transportation land

CHECK YOUR FACTS

Look at the Map

6. What is most land in the Kansas City area used for?

7. What is most of the land along the Missouri River and Kansas River used for?

8. Is there more public land north or south of the Missouri River?

Look at the Lesson

9. What does a land-use map show?

10. On what kind of land are government buildings found?

THINK ABOUT IT

How is the land used in your community?

Lesson 4: Kansas City's Central Business District

NEW WORDS

central business district

downtown

Kansas City has much industrial and residential land. But in one place in Kansas City, almost all the land is commercial land. This place is called the **central business district.** Sometimes, the central business district is called **downtown.**

Kansas City's central business district is almost in the middle of the city. It is easy to reach from all parts of the city. Find Kansas City's central business district on the map on page 95.

The central business district becomes very crowded during the day. Many workers and shoppers are there then. At night, most people go home to other parts of the city. The central

This is a view of Kansas City from an airplane.

business district is not crowded at night. It is also not crowded on Sundays and holidays.

This map shows the Kansas City area. Use the grid to find City Hall for Kansas City, Missouri. It is in square *C3*. This is also where the

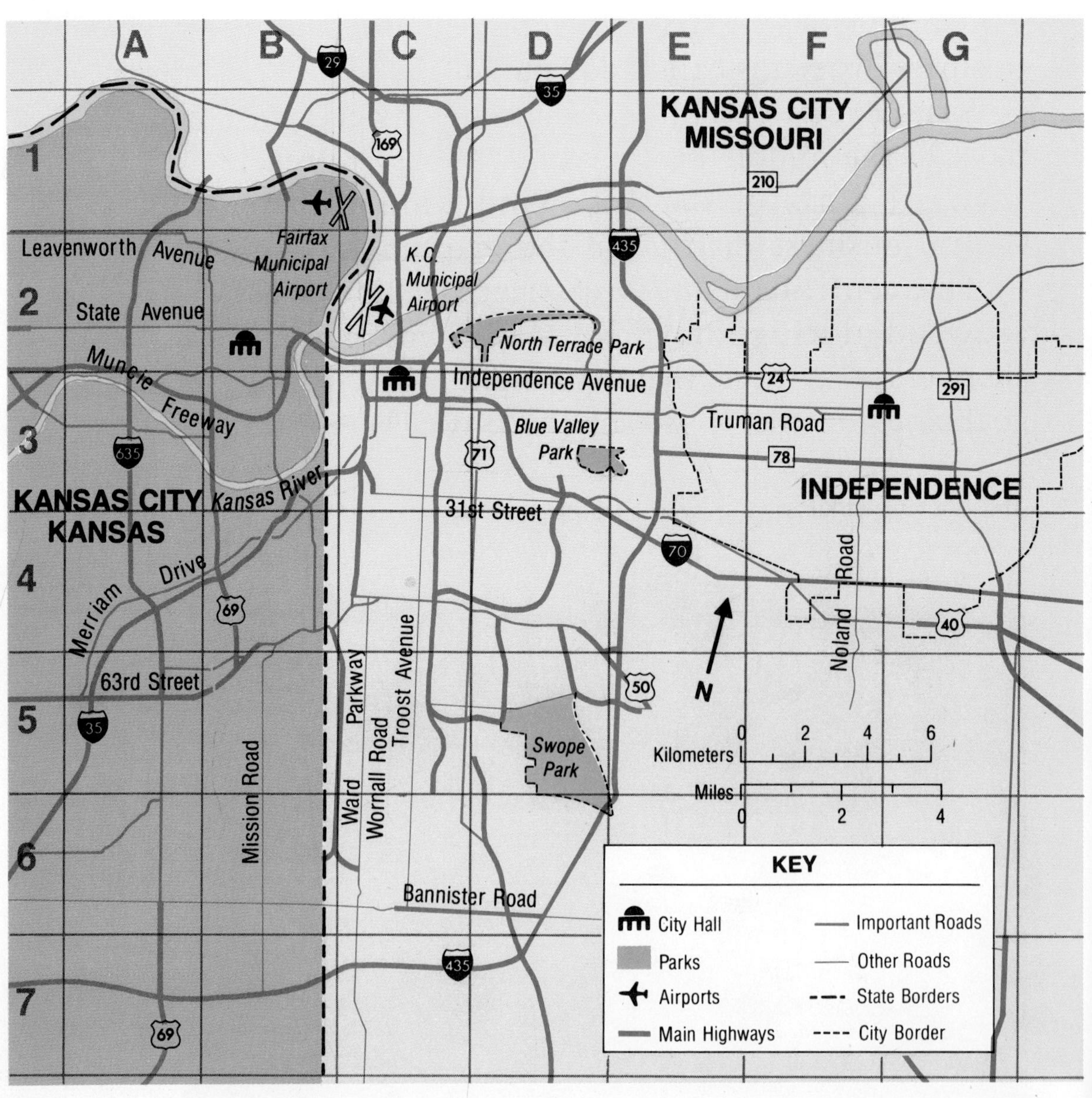

KANSAS CITY CENTRAL BUSINESS DISTRICT

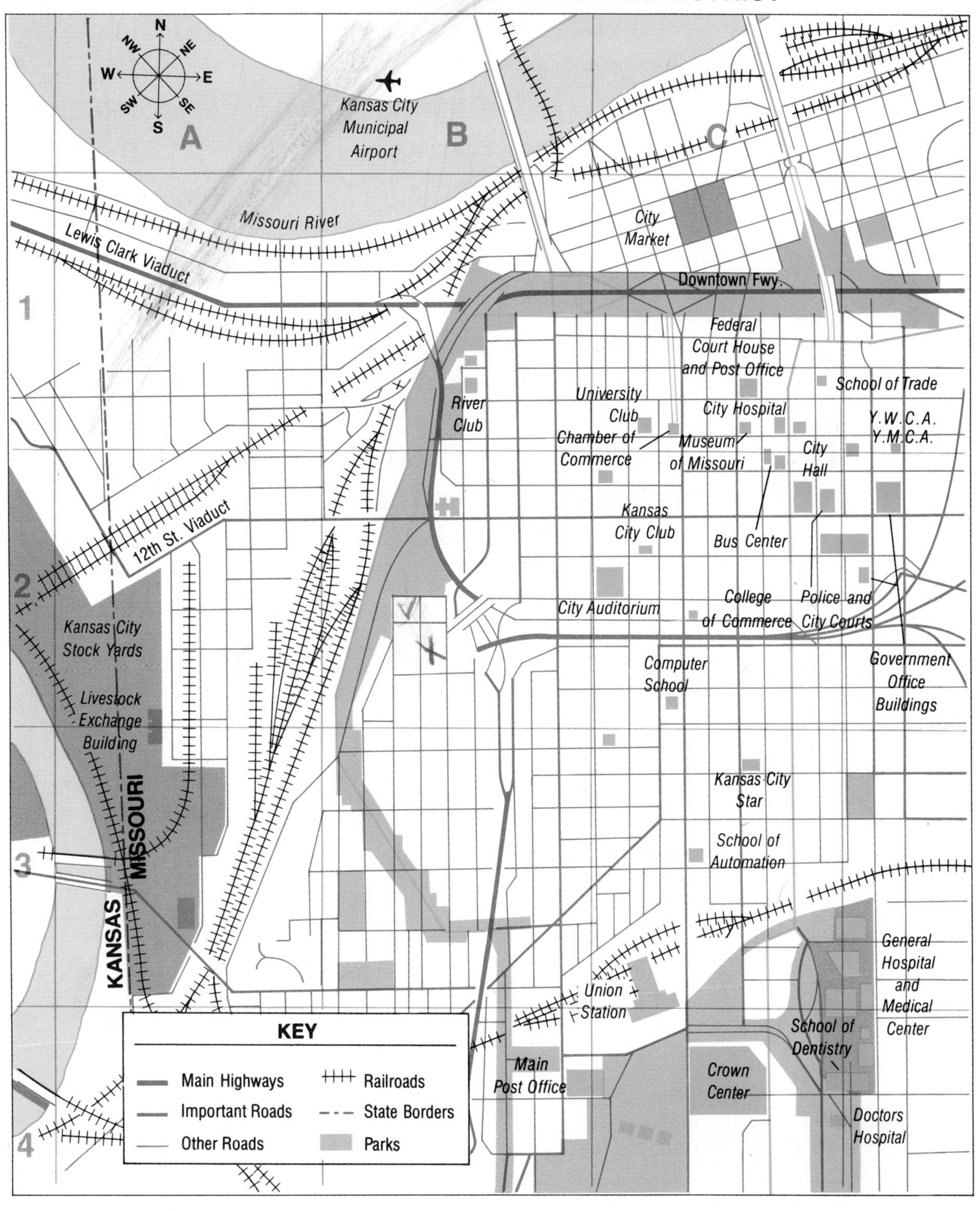

central business district is. There are many highways that go to and from the central business district.

Why do you think so many roads go to the central business district? One reason is so that people can come in to work and shop. There is another reason. Many goods must come into the central business district. Many goods are also sent out.

Look at the map on page 99. It shows the central business district of Kansas City up close. Use the grid. Look in square *C1*. The city market is there. So is a post office and a hospital. Look in square *A2*. The Kansas City stockyards are there. Now use the map key. Find the railroads and main highways. Trains and trucks go in and out of Kansas City. They bring cattle to the stockyards. They bring supplies to businesses, hospitals, and schools.

REVIEW

CHECK YOUR FACTS

Look at the Map

1. What important transportation center is in square *C3?*
2. What square is the City Auditorium in?

Look at the Lesson

3. The central business district is crowded during the (day/night).
4. Give two reasons why so many roads and railroads go into the central business district of Kansas City.

THINK ABOUT IT

Does your community have a central business district? If so, where is it? If not, have you ever visited one in another community? Where?

CHAPTER REVIEW

WATCH YOUR WORDS

1. Many people moved west in ___.
   wagon trains warehouses stockyards
2. Things are stored in a___.
   wagon train warehouse stockyard
3. Cattle are kept in___.
   wagon trains warehouses stockyards
4. The central business district is the same as___.
   downtown public land residential land
5. People live on___.
   vacant land public land residential land

CHECK YOUR FACTS

6. Who were the first people to live in the Kansas City area?
7. Which came first, the fur trade or the wagon trains?
8. Railroads (did/did not) help Kansas City grow.
9. What river does the Hannibal Bridge cross?
10. In recent years, Kansas City has become (larger/smaller).
11. What will you find if you visit commercial land?
12. On what kind of land are train stations and airports?
13. Where is Kansas City's central business district?
14. There (are/are not) many roads in Kansas City's central business district.

USE YOUR MAPS

15. Look at the map on page 89. Which was longer, the Oregon Trail or the Santa Fe Trail?
16. Look at the land-use map of Kansas City on page 95. How is most of the land used in the cities around Kansas City?
17. Look at the map on page 85. Does the Missouri River form a state border?
18. Look at the map of the Kansas City area on page 98. What two large cities border on Kansas City, Missouri?
19. Look at the map of the central business district on page 99. In what square are there two bridges?

THINK ABOUT IT

20. Why did many settlers going west travel in wagon trains?
21. Is your community growing larger, staying the same, or getting smaller?
22. Do you think all land should be used? Why, or why not?
23. In what ways is Kansas City like your community? In what ways is it different?

CHAPTER 3 GOODS AND SERVICES

Lesson 1: What Are Goods and Services?

NEW WORDS
- goods
- service
- consumer

People go to commercial areas for many reasons. One reason is to go to work. Another important reason is to get goods and services. What are goods and services?

Goods are things that you can touch, see, hear, or taste.

Here are examples of goods. Goods are the foods people eat. Goods are the clothes people wear. Goods are beds, tables, and chairs. Cars, books, and toys are all goods.

Services are different from goods. A **service** is something people do to fill the needs of other people.

Some people perform services to keep you healthy. Doctors, nurses, and dentists are some of these people. Fire fighters and police officers perform services to keep you safe. Other people perform services in your school. You know your teachers perform important services. But someone also runs the office in your school. Someone works in the library. Someone keeps the school clean. All these people perform services in your school.

People are performing a service when they serve you food. They are doing so when they fix your TV. Showing you a movie is also a service.

You can perform services, too. You can mow the lawn. You can set the table or do the dishes. You can take care of younger children.

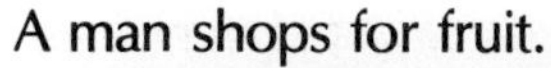

A woman delivers the mail.

A man shops for fruit.

People shop for camping gear.

People use goods, such as cars and food. They also use services. Every time people go to doctors or barbers, they are using services. People who use goods and services are called **consumers** (kun SOO murz). You use goods and services. You are a consumer, too.

REVIEW

WATCH YOUR WORDS

1. ___ are things you can touch.
   Goods Services Consumers
2. ___ are people who use things.
   Goods Services Consumers

CHECK YOUR FACTS

3. List two reasons why people go to commercial areas.
4. Foods are (goods/services).
5. Doctors and fire fighters provide (goods/services).

TRY SOMETHING NEW

On a piece of paper, write *goods* and *services.* Underneath, list all the things you can think of that you have used today. Be careful to put each thing in the right group. For example, you might list *orange juice* under *goods* and *library* under *services.*

Lesson 2: Kansas City Goods and Services

NEW WORD

tax

Workers in Kansas City make many different goods. Here are some of them. Flour and other foods are made in Kansas City. Clothes, cars, and trucks are made there. So are books and greeting cards.

Services are important to communities. So cities and towns often provide services people need. Kansas City provides many services for its people. Some of these services are like those in your community.

People need clean water. Kansas City provides water for homes and businesses.

People make trash and garbage. Kansas City must see that the trash and garbage are picked up. Then, the city must get rid of the trash and garbage.

People need to go from place to place. Kansas City provides streets and buses for the people. Kansas City has a large airport. Airplanes take people to and from the city.

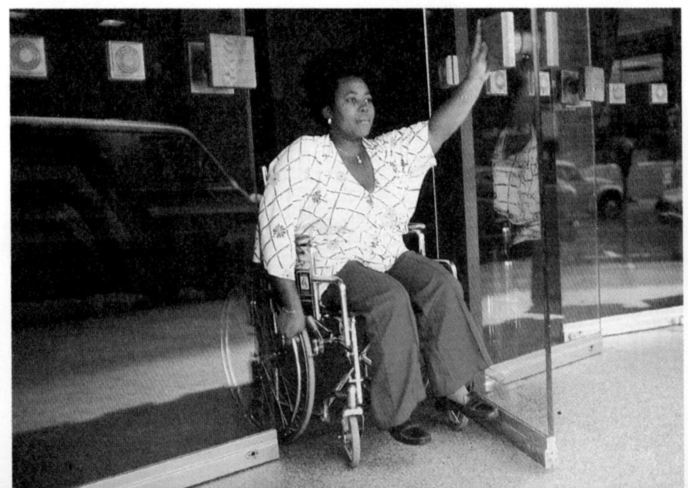

Left: Some cities make curbs with ramps for people in wheelchairs.
Below: Children enjoy the zoo.

People need to be safe from fires and criminals. Kansas City provides fire-fighting and police services.

All these services are not free. The city collects money, called **taxes,** from the people. City services are paid for with taxes.

Most communities, even small ones, provide services. But cities have more services than small communities. The larger a community is, the more services it provides.

Kansas City is large enough to have special services for its people. Kansas City has a large art gallery and a fine zoo. It has a special library of science. It has many sports, such as baseball, basketball, football, and hockey.

These kinds of services help people have fun and learn about special things. People could get along without such services.

Left: Trash is picked up regularly. *Below:* Roads often need to be repaired.

REVIEW

CHECK YOUR FACTS

1. Give three examples of goods made in Kansas City.
2. What services keep people safe?
3. The services Kansas City provides (are/are not) free.
4. Large communities tend to provide (more/fewer) services than small ones.
5. What does the city do with trash and garbage?

THINK ABOUT IT

Name some services your community provides.

CHAPTER REVIEW

WATCH YOUR WORDS

1. ___are things people use.
   Goods Taxes Consumers
2. ___are things people do.
   Goods Services Taxes
3. A city collects ___ to pay for services.
   goods services taxes

CHECK YOUR FACTS

4. People (do/do not) go to commercial land to work.
5. Books are (goods/services).
6. Teachers and police officers provide (goods/services).
7. What are people who use goods and services called?
8. Name some goods made in Kansas City.
9. Name some services Kansas City provides.
10. How are city services paid for?
11. Small communities (do/do not) provide services.

THINK ABOUT IT

12. In their work, do your parents provide goods or services?
13. List some goods and services that are provided in your neighborhood.
14. Is everyone a consumer? Why, or why not?
15. What services do you provide at home?
16. What kinds of goods and services are most important? What kinds are less important?

CHAPTER 4 MAKING A LIVING

Lesson 1: Jobs and Workers

NEW WORD

skill

People work to fill many of their needs.

Workers use the money they earn to meet their needs. Here is how they do it. Workers spend time on their jobs. They use their energy. And they use their skills. A **skill** is something a person knows how to do well. Some workers use their time, energy, and skills to make goods. Other workers perform services.

People exchange their work for money. Then, they exchange the money for goods and services they want. They pay for food and a place to live.

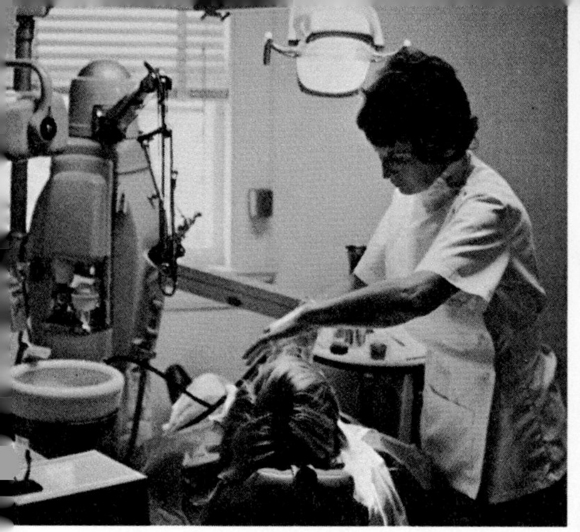

Top: A dentist takes care of people's teeth. *Right:* Fire fighters put out a fire.

They buy clothes, movie tickets, and many other things.

Jobs fill other kinds of needs, too. People spend much of their time at work. They want to be happy there. They want to do something they like. They want to be proud of what they can do.

REVIEW

CHECK YOUR FACTS

1. How do people fill many of their needs?
2. What three things do workers use on a job?
3. What do people get in return for their work?
4. Jobs (do/do not) fill needs other than for money.

THINK ABOUT IT

What kinds of work do your parents do? What kinds of skills do they have?

Lesson 2: Wants and Costs

NEW WORD

cost

Everyone has wants. People want many things. But most of the time they cannot have everything they want. They may not have enough money. They may not have enough time. So people must choose the things they want most. They must give up other things.

Every time you choose one thing, you give up something else.

Suppose you have a dollar. You choose to buy a movie ticket. You must give your money for the ticket.

But the movie costs you more than just money. What if you wanted a comic book, too? Giving up the comic book is part of what the movie costs you.

When you mow someone's lawn, you get money for it. But cutting the grass also costs you something. It costs you your time and energy. Time and energy are costs.

This glove has the right fit.

A boy buys a ticket for the movies.

Suppose you have two friends. One wants to play baseball. The other wants to go swimming. Each one wants you to go with her. What do you do? You cannot be in both places at the same-time. When you choose to play baseball, you give up swimming. The cost of playing baseball with one friend is not going swimming with the other.

The **cost** of something is what you give up for it. Cost includes all the things you give up when you make a choice.

REVIEW

CHECK YOUR FACTS

1. People usually (can/cannot) have everything they want.
2. When you choose one thing, what do you also do?
3. When you buy something, money (is/is not) your only cost.
4. What does work such as mowing a lawn cost you?

THINK ABOUT IT

Often, it is hard to choose one thing and give up something else. Give an example of something you chose. What was the cost?

Lesson 3: Consumers Choose

NEW WORDS

- decision model
- problem
- choice
- result
- decision

Look at the drawing below. It is called a **decision model.** This is a drawing that shows one way people decide things. Here is how to read the drawing: First, there is a **problem.** This is something to be solved. There are different ways to solve a problem. These are the **choices.** For every problem, you have to figure out what the choices are. Then, you have to figure out what will happen if you make each choice. What will happen is called the **result.** Let's try out the model.

Joan and Ted Reed both have jobs. With the money they earn, they buy things their family needs. Then, they have money left over. The Reeds want to decide how to use this money.

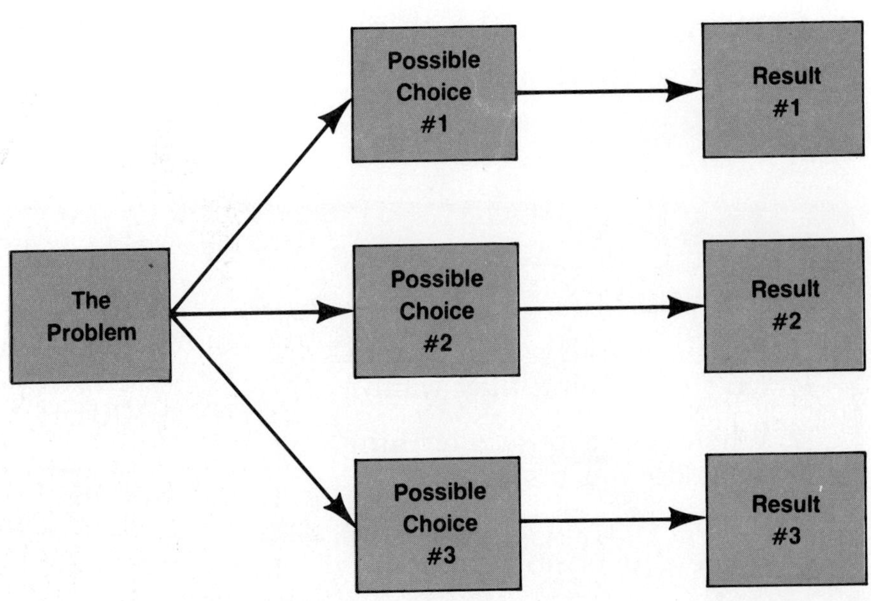

They have a few choices. They can save the money. They can spend it. Or they can spend some of the money and save the rest.

The Reeds think about the results of each choice. Suppose they save the money. Then, the family might be able to take a trip together.

Suppose they spend the money now. Then, they can have the TV fixed. And they can buy baseball gloves for Carol and Bob. The children are on a neighborhood team.

Suppose the Reeds save part of the money. Then, they can still plan for a trip. They can spend the rest of the money on one thing they want right now. They can have the TV fixed. Or they can buy the baseball gloves. But there will not be enough money to do both.

The Reeds think about the results of each choice. They think about what is most important to them. Then they make a **decision,** or final choice. What do you think the Reeds decide?

People shop for things they need and want in supermarkets and shopping centers.

REVIEW

WATCH YOUR WORDS

1. A ___ can help you decide things.
   cost tax decision model
2. A ___ is what happens after you make a choice.
   decision result problem
3. A___is a final choice.
   decision cost problem
4. A ___ is something to be solved.
   choice model problem

CHECK YOUR FACTS

5. In what way can you show how people decide things?
6. What are the different ways to solve a problem called?

TRY SOMETHING NEW

Suppose you have $5. What will you do with it? Draw a decision model. Show at least three possible choices. Show the results of each choice.

CHAPTER REVIEW

WATCH YOUR WORDS

1. A(n) ___ is something a person knows how to do well.
   occupation skill problem
2. The ___ of something is what you give up for it.
   cost choice result
3. A___is something to be solved.
   decision result problem
4. A___is a final choice.
   problem decision cost

CHECK YOUR FACTS

5. What three things do workers use on a job?
6. What do people get in return for their work?
7. What happens when you choose one thing?
8. Most of the time, people (can/cannot) have everything they want.
9. What is a decision model?
10. What are the three parts of a decision model?

THINK ABOUT IT

11. People earn money when they work. Often, they enjoy their work and are proud of it. Which do you think is more important, the money or the other rewards? Give reasons for your answer.
12. What costs are involved when you go to a movie?
13. What kind of job would you like to do when you grow up?

CHAPTER 5 OUR NATION'S ENERGY CAPITAL

Lesson 1: Transportation and Energy

NEW WORDS

means of transportation
engine
energy
fuel
petroleum
oil

Houston is the biggest city in Texas. It is the fifth-largest city in our nation. But Houston is important for many other reasons as well. Houston is often called our nation's energy capital. In this chapter, we are going to study Houston. We are also going to learn about transportation and energy. Find Houston on the map on page 85.

Have you ever gone to visit relatives far away? Did you ever get a package in the mail? You know that people are always going from place to place. People send goods from place to place, too. People use cars, trucks, trains, airplanes, and boats to travel. They send goods in the same way. The ways that people and goods

Early railroad trains roar down the tracks.

move from place to place are called **means of transportation.**

For a long time, people walked wherever they went. Walking was their only means of transportation. Later, they may have ridden a horse. Or they might have ridden on a wagon pulled by a horse or other animal. They sent goods the same way. On water, they traveled in boats. They moved the boats with oars or sails.

Then, about 150 years ago, transportation began to change. Engines were used to move boats on water. They were used to pull loads on the ground. Because these engines were so heavy, they were put on iron tracks. This new means of transportation was called the railroad.

Engines are machines. They use energy to do things that are useful to people. We will talk about energy a little later. Over the years, people made better and better engines. Today, we use many engines in transportation. Small engines move motor bikes. Large engines move cars and trucks. Huge engines move trains and airplanes. The biggest engines push ships across the oceans.

All these engines help move people and goods. They help people get the things they need. They help people get things when they want them.

All engines run on **energy.** One kind of energy is heat. Heat is made by burning **fuel.** One of the most important fuels today is petroleum. **Petroleum** is a dark, thick liquid like thin mud. It is

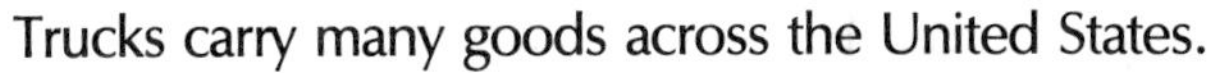
Trucks carry many goods across the United States.

found deep under the ground. It is sometimes called **oil.**

People drill holes deep into the earth to find petroleum. When they find it, they pump it to the surface. From it, people make many useful products. They make gasoline for cars and fuels for trucks and airplanes. They make fuel oil to heat homes and to make electricity. They can use petroleum to make plastics, carpets, clothing, records, and chemicals. These are only some of the ways that petroleum can be used.

Petroleum is our most important source of energy. Houston is the center of the petroleum business in the United States. Thus, it is our nation's energy capital.

REVIEW

WATCH YOUR WORDS

1. ___ are machines that use energy to do useful things.
Horses Fuels Engines

2. Heat is made by burning___.
energy fuel engines

3. Heat is one kind of___.
energy fuel engine

4. ___ is the same as oil.
Energy Fuel Petroleum

5. The ways that people move from place to place are called___.
means of transportation
fuel engines

CHECK YOUR FACTS

6. What city is often called our nation's energy capital?

7. Name some things people use to travel and send goods.

8. At first, how did people move from place to place?

9. What began to be used in transportation about 150 years ago?.

10. What do all engines run on?

11. Where is petroleum found?

THINK ABOUT IT

What means of transportation have you used today?

Lesson 2: Houston Is Founded

Americans began moving from the United States to Texas in the early 1800s. Texas was then part of Mexico. In 1821, the Mexican government gave Stephen F. Austin, an American, land for 3000 settlers. Other settlers followed. Soon, the Mexican government began to worry. Too many Americans were coming to their land. In 1830, there were 20,000 Americans in eastern Texas. The Mexican government said that no more could come. But the Mexicans and Americans no longer trusted each other. The Americans in Texas came to think of themselves as Texans.

In 1835, fighting broke out between the Mexicans and the Texans, A year later, on March 2, 1836, the Texans declared Texas an independent nation. A war followed.

Davy Crockett, with the gun over his head, and other Texans fight the Mexicans.

General Santa Anna surrenders to Sam Houston. Houston, who is lying down, was wounded in the battle.

One famous battle of this war took place at the Alamo. The Alamo is a building in downtown San Antonio. But back then, it was used as a fort by the Texans. About 182 soldiers were at the Alamo on February 23, 1836. Among them were Davy Crockett, Jim Bowie, and Bill Travis. On that day, the Alamo was surrounded by a Mexican army of several thousand soldiers. Its leader was General Santa Anna.

For 10 days, the Mexicans fired cannons at the Alamo. Then, on the 10th day, they charged. Twice, the Texans turned them back. On their third try, the Mexicans stormed the walls. The Texans fought bravely. But all were killed.

Later, General Santa Anna and his army marched to a place called San Jacinto (SAN hah

SIN toh). This was near where the city of Houston is today. Santa Anna intended to catch the Texas army there. He hoped to destroy it. He thought the Texans had given up.

But the Texans surprised Santa Anna. On April 21, 1836, Santa Anna gave his troops the afternoon to rest. They were not ready to fight. Suddenly, the Texans attacked. Led by Sam Houston, they defeated part of Santa Anna's army. The Texans captured Santa Anna. To free himself, he agreed to let Texas become independent. So, Texas became the Republic of Texas. It was called the Lone Star Republic. Its flag had only one star. Sam Houston became the first elected president of the republic. He had once been the governor of the state of Tennessee. Texas did not become part of the United States until 1845.

Two brothers, Austin and John Allen, founded Houston in August 1836. They named it after the president of the republic. Until 1839, it was the capital of the republic.

REVIEW

CHECK YOUR FACTS

1. What nation once owned the land where Houston is?
2. What American was given land in Texas for settlers?
3. What famous battle did the Texans lose?
4. Who led the Texans at San Jacinto?

THINK ABOUT IT

The southwestern part of the United States once belonged to Mexico. Was the land of your state ever Mexican?

Lesson 3: Houston Grows

NEW WORDS

- oil field
- natural gas
- oil tanker
- ship channel
- refinery
- petrochemical
- port

For many years explorers had been looking for petroleum in Texas. They had drilled some small wells. Then, in 1901, there was much excitement in Houston. Oil! Black gold, it was called! Petroleum had been discovered at Spindletop in eastern Texas. The amount of petroleum was huge. Thousands of barrels flowed from the well every day.

Soon, oil companies drilled many other wells in the oil field. Areas where petroleum is found are called **oil fields.** People found several big oil fields in eastern Texas. **Natural gas** came out of the ground with the petroleum. Today, natural gas is the fuel burned in most stoves in the United States.

Houston had a good location. It was in the middle of the United States. It was near the Gulf of Mexico. It could become a center for the petroleum and gas business. But first, a problem had to be solved.

Houston is 80 kilometers (50 miles) from the Gulf of Mexico. The city needed a water route to the sea. Buffalo Bayou flowed from Houston to the Gulf of Mexico. But it was a small stream. It was not wide or deep enough for big ships. Yet, petroleum is often moved by large ships, called **oil tankers.**

Leaders of Houston figured out how to solve the problem. They needed to make Buffalo Bayou wider and deeper. That way, they could make it into a **ship channel.** This is a water route that people dig for ships to use. The ship channel would connect Houston with the Gulf of Mexico. Then, big ships could reach Houston from the ocean. The ship channel was finally finished in 1914. The United States government helped pay for it. Then many new businesses began to move to the Houston area. Many oil refineries were built near Houston.

Refineries are big factories that make petroleum useful. They break it down into parts. Refineries can get gasoline from petroleum. They can get fuel for trucks and airplanes. They can get oil for heat. They can get asphalt for paving streets. All of these things can come from the same barrel of petroleum.

Oil companies need pipes and drills. They need big trucks. They need other things made from iron and steel. Many businesses selling these kinds of products came to Houston.

Big ships are unloaded in the port of Houston.

Top: The Johnson Space Center is named for President Lyndon B. Johnson.
Right: Houston has many oil refineries.

Houston also became a center for petrochemicals (PET roh KEM i kulz). **Petrochemicals** are chemicals made from petroleum and natural gas. Many different kinds of plastics are made from petrochemicals. Petrochemicals are also used to make other products, such as cloth.

With all these new businesses, Houston grew more. By 1930, Houston was the largest city in Texas. It had almost 300,000 people.

Houston grew even faster during the 1940s and 1950s. New factories were built in and near the city. They made chemicals, machines, and rubber. Then, in the early 1960s, the Johnson Space Center was started in Houston. That brought more new businesses to the city. Houston became known as Space City. When astronauts are in space, they keep in touch with Earth through Houston.

Today, Houston has almost 2 million people. It supplies the United States with over half its petrochemicals. It supplies most of the rubber used in tires. It is the third-busiest port in the United States. A **port** is a place where ships load and unload goods. Houston has many companies that do business all over the world. Companies from Houston help other companies drill for petroleum in the ocean. They make special drills for this. They know what to do when accidents happen.

Houston also has many other important services. It has many fine hospitals. It has several famous colleges. It has big banks. Houston also has sports teams. They play in the Astrodome. It is a huge enclosed stadium.

Houston has grown very fast. This growth has caused some problems. You will read about them in the next lesson.

Sports can be played indoors in the Houston Astrodome.

FUN FACTS

Petroleum is used for fuel to run cars, trucks, and planes. But it also has many other uses. Oil is used to keep machines and engines running. Oil is placed on the different parts of a machine. The oil keeps those parts from wearing out.

Petrochemicals are used in making many things that are part of everyday life. Petrochemicals are used in making paint, ink, wax, and cloth. They are used in face makeup. Petrochemicals are used in making dyes that turn cloth different colors. They are used in pills we take when we are sick. And they are even in food we eat every day. Petroleum and petrochemicals have become an important part of the way we live.

REVIEW

WATCH YOUR WORDS

1. Areas where petroleum is found are called ___.
channels refineries
oil fields

2. ___ are factories that make petroleum useful.
Oil tankers Refineries
Oil fields

3. Ships load and unload goods in a(n)___.
oil tanker petrochemical
port

4. ___ are made from oil and natural gas.
Ship channels
Petrochemicals Ports

CHECK YOUR FACTS

5. Where was petroleum discovered in 1901?

6. How was Houston connected by water with the Gulf of Mexico?

7. How do refineries make petroleum useful?

8. How did Houston come to be called Space City?

9. Where do Houston's sports teams play?

THINK ABOUT IT

Is any petroleum or natural gas produced in your area?

Lesson 4: An Unplanned City

NEW WORDS

zoning laws
freeways

Today, Houston is a big, growing city. Each year, its businesses create more jobs. Each year, more people move to Houston to get jobs. These people need homes and schools. They need stores to shop in and roads to ride on.

The growth of Houston was not planned. Leaders of the city government did not want to tell business leaders what to do. So they did not pass zoning laws in Houston. **Zoning laws** say what land in cities can be used for.

You read in the last chapter about the plan for using land in Kansas City. There, land in some zones, or areas, is supposed to be residential. The law says that only houses or apartment buildings can be built there. Other land is commercial or industrial. There, businesses and factories can be built. But Houston has no such zoning laws for its land. People can build anything they like anywhere they like.

Almost everyone uses freeways to get around Houston.

Some people in Houston say the lack of zoning has been good for the city. Many businesses, factories, and homes have been built.

Other people say the lack of zoning has been bad for the city. They say that beautiful parts of the city have been ruined. Factories can be built right in the middle of a neighborhood.

Houston is very spread out. City leaders have tried to connect all parts of the city together. They have done this with freeways. **Freeways** are big roads that cost nothing to use. Almost everyone who lives in Houston must travel by car. There are few buses and no trains or trolley cars. So there is much automobile traffic. This traffic often crawls along very slowly.

The leaders of Houston know about the city's problems. They intend to solve them. In the past, Houston's leaders helped the city grow. They also helped the city solve its problems.

REVIEW

WATCH YOUR WORDS

1. Houston has no____.
   zoning laws freeways port
2. Houston is connected by____.
   zoning refining freeways

CHECK YOUR FACTS

3. The growth of Houston (was/was not) planned.
4. It (does/does not) cost money to ride on a freeway.
5. How do most people get around in Houston?

TRY SOMETHING NEW

Find out from a leader in your community if your community has zoning laws.

CHAPTER REVIEW

WATCH YOUR WORDS

1. ___ are machines that use energy to do useful things.
   Tankers Fuels Engines
2. Heat is made by burning___.
   energy fuel refineries
3. Petroleum is the same as___.
   energy oil natural gas
4. ___are made from petroleum.
   Petrochemicals Refineries Natural gases
5. A(n) ___ connects Houston to the Gulf of Mexico.
   oil tanker refinery ship channel
6. Goods are loaded and unloaded in___.
   freeways ports engines
7. ___are big roads.
   Freeways Ports Ship channels
8. Oil tankers are a___.
   means of transportation zoning law ship channel
9. Petroleum is made useful in a(n)___.
   oil tanker refinery oil field

CHECK YOUR FACTS

10. What is the biggest city in Texas?
11. What is our nation's most important source of energy?
12. With what nation did the Texans fight a war?
13. For whom is the city of Houston named?
14. Houston's growth has been (planned/unplanned).

THINK ABOUT IT

15. You have probably used a number of different means of transportation. Name as many as you can.
16. Many American cities have Spanish names. List as many as you can think of.
17. Do you think we will always have plenty of oil and natural gas? Why, or why not?
18. Do you think there should be zoning laws? Give reasons for your answer.

UNIT REVIEW

WATCH YOUR WORDS

Use the words below to fill in the blanks. Use each term only once.

boundary	lakes	petrochemicals	services
downtown	means of transportation	petroleum	ship channel
energy	natural gas	plains	skills
engines	oil fields	port	stockyards
fuel	oil tankers	refineries	taxes
goods		river	wagon trains

In the Middle United States, there are large areas of flat land called___. The most important___ in the area is the Mississippi. In the north, five large___form part of the___with Canada.

Kansas City is an important city in the Middle United States. Long ago, there was a trading post there. Later,___left there for the West. Cattle were shipped to Kansas City, and the___were built. Today, Kansas City has a busy___ with many tall buildings. There, businesses sell___and provide___. The city also provides services. The people of Kansas City pay for city services with___. The people who work in Kansas City have many different___.

Houston is another important city in the Middle United States. It is often called our nation's___ capital. Today, people burn___in ___ to get energy. This provides power for different___that people use to get around and move things. Our nation's most important source of energy is___.

Houston is a center of the oil business. Petroleum and another fuel,___, are found there in areas called___. Large ships, called___, carry the petroleum. They use the ___ to get from Houston to the Gulf of Mexico. Thus, though it is inland, Houston is an important ___. The city has huge___ that make petroleum useful. ___ are also made in Houston.

CHECK YOUR FACTS

1. What two mountain ranges border the Middle United States?
2. What do you use to find directions on a map?
3. What do you use to find distance on a map?
4. What two rivers meet at Kansas City?
5. Name two means of transportation used in Kansas City.

6. What does a land-use map show you?
7. Where in Kansas City is almost all the commercial land?
8. List three kinds of buildings found on public land.
9. What two kinds of things do consumers use?
10. Kansas City provides (many/few) services.
11. Why do people work?
12. What does *cost* mean?
13. What do you call a drawing that shows how people decide things?
14. Why is Houston often called our nation's energy capital?
15. Petroleum (is/is not) used just as it comes from the ground.
16. What are freeways?
17. In Houston, people (can/cannot) build anything anywhere.

CLOSE THE MAP GAP

18. Draw a map of your state. Put the state capital, large cities, and important bodies of water on the map. Include a compass and a distance scale.

USE YOUR MAPS

Use the map of the Middle United States on page 85 to answer questions 19–21.

19. List the Great Lakes shown on the map.
20. Suppose you are in Frankfort, Kentucky. In what direction is Nashville, Tennessee?
21. Measure Kansas from north to south. How wide is Kansas? Then measure Kansas from west to east. How long is Kansas? Give your answers in kilometers and miles.
22. Look at the land-use map of Kansas City on page 95. Is there more industrial land north or south of the Missouri River?
23. Look at the map of the Kansas City central business district on page 99. Is Crown Center north or south of City Hall?

THINK ABOUT IT

24. Name some things that can make a city grow. What other things might make people leave a city?
25. List as many sources of energy as you can.
26. You have probably used many things today that are made from petroleum. List as many as you can.

TRY SOMETHING NEW

27. Draw a decision model about a choice you may have to make concerning money.

THE WESTERN UNITED STATES

UNIT 3

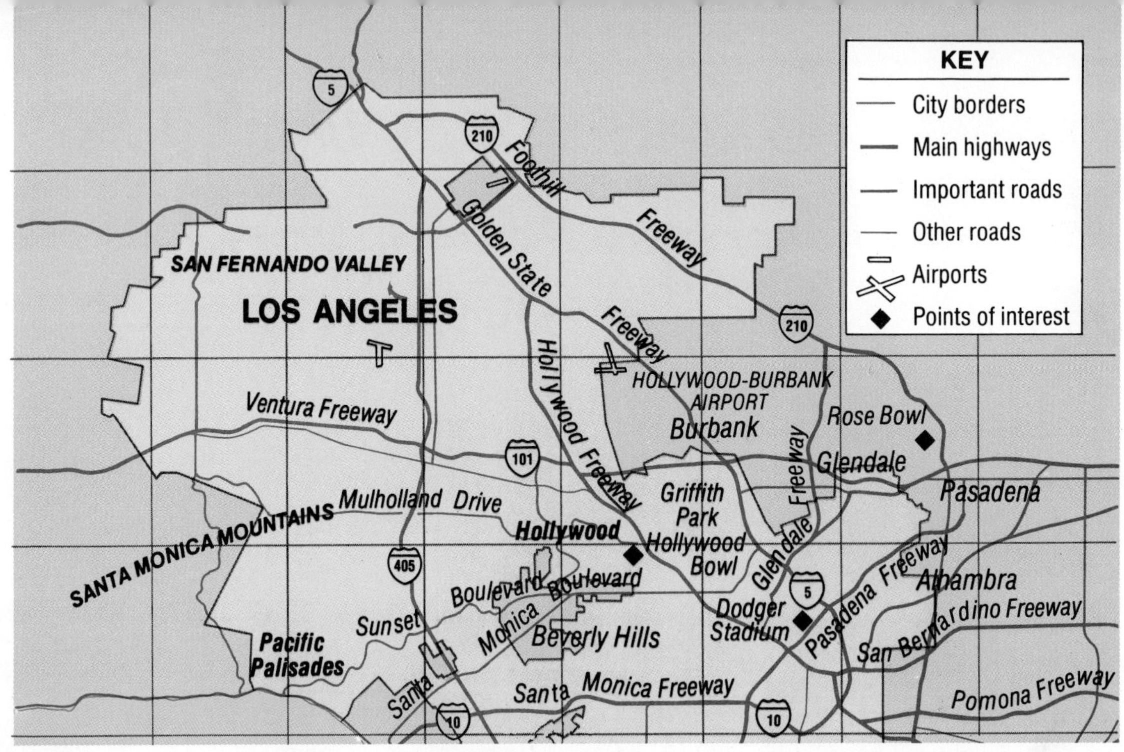

CHAPTER 1 LEARNING FROM MAPS AND GRAPHS

Lesson 1: Mapping the Western United States

NEW WORDS

island

desert

In this unit, you will learn much about the city of Los Angeles. Los Angeles is in the Western United States, or the West. This is the area between the Rocky Mountains and the Pacific Ocean.

Look at the map of the Western United States on page 136. Find the Rocky Mountains on the map. Then, find the Pacific Ocean. Eleven American states lie between these giant mountains and the ocean. Washington and Oregon are two of those states. Can you name the others?

The states of Hawaii and Alaska are also shown on the map. But they are not really part of the land area we call the Western United States. Hawaii is a group of islands in the Pacific Ocean. An **island** is an area of land surrounded by water on all sides. Look at a globe. Find Hawaii in the Pacific Ocean. Find Alaska next to Canada in the north. In this unit, you will also study Honolulu, the capital of Hawaii.

There are several mountain ranges in the Western United States. The Rocky Mountains are the largest range in North America. They begin in Alaska and end in the state of New Mexico.

Along the Pacific Coast are two other mountain ranges. They are the Cascade Mountains and the Sierra (see EHR uh) Nevada. Between these mountains and the Rocky Mountains is a large area called the Great Basin. The land there is flat and very dry. The Great Basin is one of several deserts in the West. A **desert** is a place that gets very little rain.

In the state of Utah is the Great Salt Lake. There is something special about the Great Salt Lake. It is very salty. Most other lakes in the world have water that is not salty.

Rivers are very important in the Western United States. In the middle and southern areas, the land is very dry. The rivers carry water needed for farming. They are an important source of water for the cities. The Colorado

WESTERN UNITED STATES

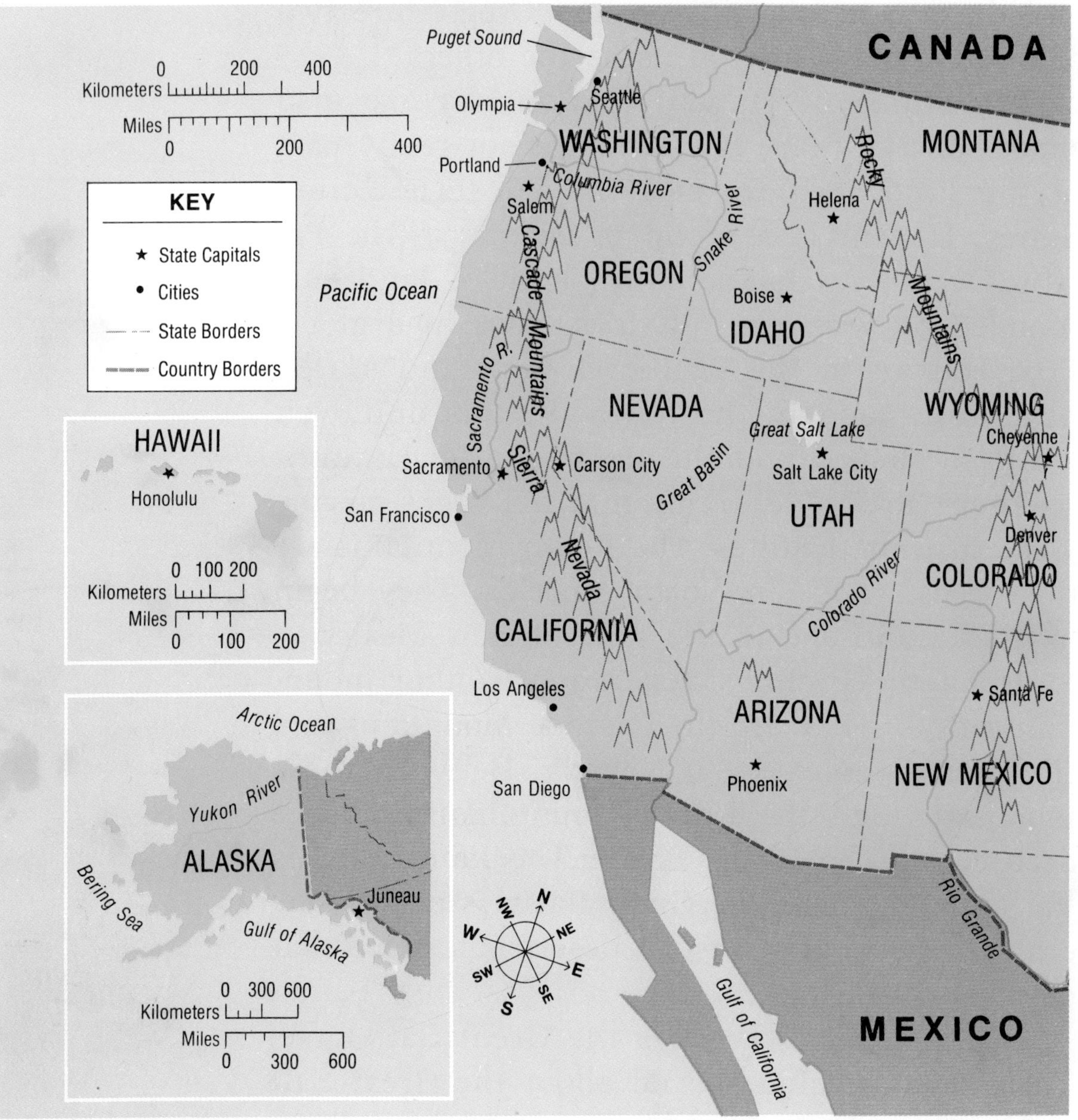

River is very long. It flows through or past five states. Look at your map. Find the Colorado River. Where does it begin? Find the Columbia River and the Sacramento River. They are important, too.

REVIEW

CHECK YOUR FACTS

Look at the Map

1. What is the name of the capital of California?
2. What river flows into the Columbia River?

Look at the Lesson

3. The Western United States lies between mountains and an ocean. What are they?
4. What two mountain ranges run along the Pacific Coast?
5. Most lakes have water that is (not salty/salty).

THINK ABOUT IT

Are there any islands or deserts near where you live? If so, what are their names?

Lesson 2: Natural Environments of California

NEW WORDS

natural environment

seacoast

valley

Los Angeles is in California. California is a large state in the Western United States.

California is special in several ways. At almost any time of year, you can swim at a beach. At the same time, you can go skiing in the mountains. You can find thick green forests in the north. You can drive through long stretches of desert land. These are some of the great differences in California's natural environments.

Your environment is made up of all the things around you. The **natural environment** of a place includes the shape and location of the land. It includes the weather. It also includes the plants and animals.

Valleys, mountains, and deserts are part of California's natural environments.

NATURAL ENVIRONMENTS OF CALIFORNIA

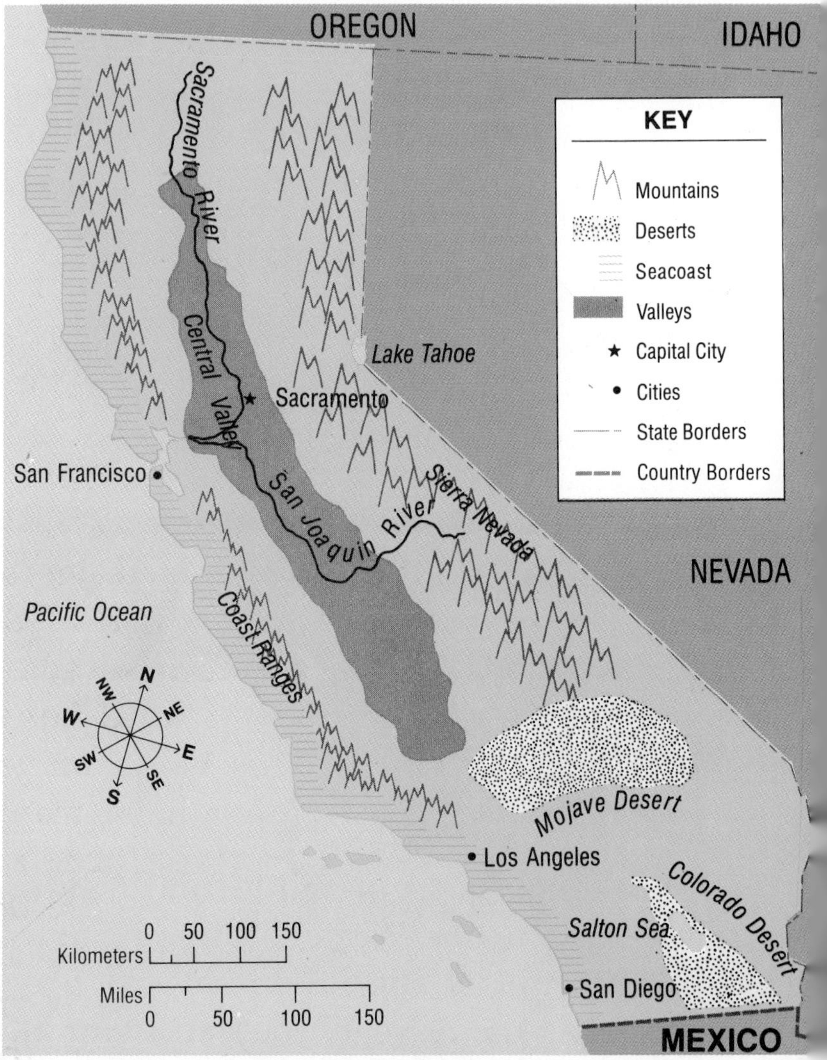

OREGON
IDAHO
NEVADA
MEXICO
Pacific Ocean
Sacramento River
Central Valley
San Joaquin River
Sierra Nevada
Coast Ranges
Lake Tahoe
Sacramento
San Francisco
Los Angeles
San Diego
Salton Sea
Mojave Desert
Colorado Desert
N NE E SE S SW W NW

KEY
Mountains
Deserts
Seacoast
Valleys
★ Capital City
• Cities
State Borders
Country Borders

Kilometers 0 50 100 150
Miles 0 50 100 150

The **seacoast** is the land closest to the ocean. California has sandy beaches in the south. There, the air is clear and warm most of the time. In the north, waves crash against great, rocky cliffs. The weather is often windy, foggy, and cool.

Next to the seacoast are low mountains. They are covered with bushes and trees. Large and beautiful redwood trees grow on these mountains in the north. These trees need the wetness of the fog near the coast.

In the eastern part of California are the Sierra Nevada. This is a range of high mountains. In the winter, these mountains are often covered with snow. There are fish in the many lakes and streams of the Sierra Nevada.

Valleys are low areas of land between the mountains. Find the Central Valley on your map. The Central Valley does not have many forests or hills. The land is very flat. There are many farms in the Central Valley. There are onion and lettuce fields. Some parts of the valley are crowded with fruit trees. The fruit is grown for sale. There is little rain in summer in the valley. Farmers get water from nearby rivers. The rivers flow down from the mountains.

The deserts in California can be very hot and dry. But some plants have found ways to live without much water. A giant cactus can store water after a rain. Other plants send long roots deep into the soil to find water. Beautiful flowers sometimes bloom in the Mojave (muh HAH vee) Desert.

REVIEW

CHECK YOUR FACTS

Look at the Map

1. What rivers flow through the Central Valley?
2. Name the two large deserts.

Look at the Lesson

3. California's natural environments are (alike/different).
4. What is the seacoast like in northern California?
5. The Central Valley is very (flat/hilly).

THINK ABOUT IT

Is the area where you live like any of the environments discussed in this lesson? If so, which one? If not, what is your area like?

Lesson 3: Urban Areas of California

California has many communities. Some are very close to one another. As you have learned, communities like these form an urban area. In an urban area, the smaller communities are usually grouped around a big city.

The map on page 141 shows the main urban areas found in California. Most urban areas have very large populations.

Look at the chart on page 141. It gives the population of some urban areas in California.

An urban area is formed as the main city grows in population. Some of the people in the city move to smaller communities nearby. They may want to get away from the older areas of the city. They may want to be less crowded. But they want to stay close to the city's jobs and services.

URBAN AREAS OF CALIFORNIA

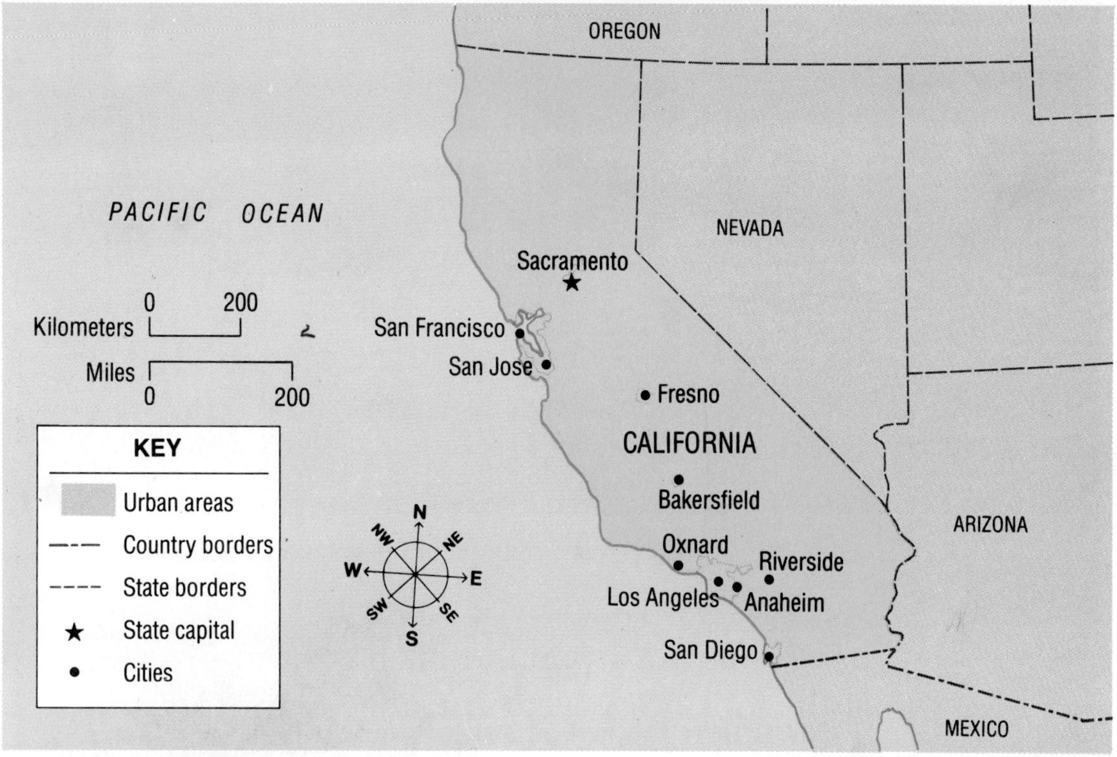

CALIFORNIA URBAN AREAS

Urban Area	Number of people	Urban Area	Number of people
Los Angeles	7,400,000	San Jose	1,300,000
San Francisco	3,200,000	Sacramento	1,000,000
Anaheim	1,900,000	Oxnard	500,000
San Diego	1,900,000	Fresno	500,000
Riverside	1,500,000	Bakersfield	400,000

As you know, the newer communities around a big city are called suburbs. People from the suburbs come to work, shop, learn, and have fun in the city. City people also visit the suburbs. Good transportation is very important in an urban area.

From the air, you can see ribbons of freeways and rows of houses.

California's population has been growing rapidly for many years. Each year, thousands of people move there. They go to get jobs and to enjoy California's good weather. Some parts of California are becoming very crowded. One such area is Los Angeles.

REVIEW

CHECK YOUR FACTS

1. What is usually at the center of an urban area?
2. Most urban areas have (large/small) populations.
3. When does an urban area form?
4. What are the newer communities around a big city called?
5. List three things that people come to the city to do.
6. Good transportation (is/is not) important in urban areas.

THINK ABOUT IT

Do you live in an urban area? If not, what is the nearest one? What is it like?

CHAPTER REVIEW

WATCH YOUR WORDS

1. A(n) ___ is a place that gets very little rain.
   island desert valley
2. A(n) ___ is an area of land surrounded by water.
   island seacoast valley
3. ___ are low areas of land between mountains.
   Natural environments
   Seacoasts Valleys
4. The ___ is the land closest to the ocean.
   natural environment seacoast desert
5. The ___ of California are very different from one another.
   natural environments islands deserts

CHECK YOUR FACTS

6. Name a state made up of islands in the Pacific Ocean.
7. What nation is Alaska next to?
8. What is the largest mountain range in North America?
9. Name a lake in Utah.
10. What state is Los Angeles in?
11. Farming (is/is not) important in the Central Valley.
12. In the Mojave Desert, flowers (sometimes/never) bloom.
13. How is an urban area formed?
14. California's population is growing (larger/smaller).

USE YOUR MAPS AND CHART

15. Look at the map of the Western United States on page 136. What is the capital of Arizona?
16. What river runs through New Mexico?
17. Look at the map of California's natural environments on page 138. Name a large lake that is on the border of California and Nevada.
18. Look at the map of California urban areas on page 141. What urban area seems to be the largest in size?
19. Look at the chart of California urban areas on page 141. What is the largest urban area in population?

THINK ABOUT IT

20. Is there a lake near where you live? If so, what is it called?
21. Why is it possible to swim and ski at the same time of the year in California?
22. Mountains can block clouds carrying rain. How does this fact help explain the deserts in California?
23. Why are there no large urban areas in eastern California?
24. What part of the Western United States would you like to visit? Why?

CHAPTER 2 THE HISTORY OF LOS ANGELES

Lesson 1: El Pueblo

NEW WORDS

pueblo
mestizo
plaza
mission

In 1781, 11 families moved to the place where Los Angeles is today. There were 46 people in all. They came from Spanish **pueblos** (PWEB lohz), or towns, in Mexico. Some of the new settlers were Spanish. There were also American Indian and Black settlers in the group. Most were **mestizos** (meh STEE zohz). These are people who are part Spanish and part American Indian.

Today, a trip from Mexico to Los Angeles takes 2 or 3 hours by plane. In 1781, it took the Los Angeles pioneers 7 months! They traveled on foot and horses. Mules carried their belongings. They brought soap, seeds, pots for cooking, axes, plows, and other tools. They also brought some cows, chickens, and pigs.

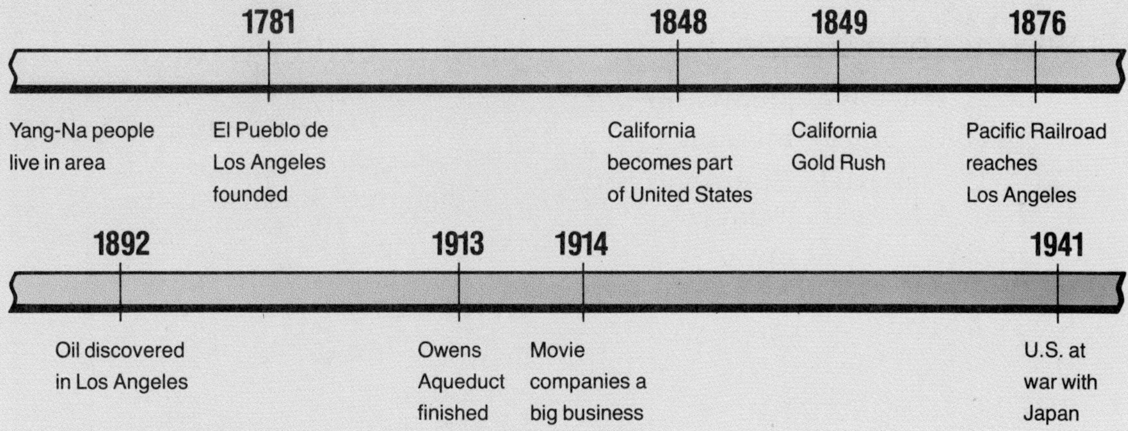

Over the next few years, the 11 families built El Pueblo de Los Angeles. This means "The Town of the Angels." They built brick houses for themselves. They made bricks of clay. Then they dried the bricks in the sun. They planted corn in their fields. Around a **plaza**, or town square, they built buildings important to the town. They built a government house, a church, and a jail. They built a large building for keeping grain and other foods.

There were American Indians in the Los Angeles area when the Spanish came. They were the Yang-na (YAN NAH) people. Some of the Yang-na went to work at a nearby **mission**, or religious settlement. They worked in the fields growing grains, oranges, and grapes. Some worked with cattle and became cowhands.

After a few years, the Yang-na went away. The Spanish wanted their lands. The Yang-na were forced to leave their villages. Most went into the mountains and deserts.

REVIEW

WATCH YOUR WORDS

1. A___is a town square.
   pueblo plaza mission
2. A ___ is part Spanish and part American Indian.
   pueblo plaza mestizo
3. A___is a Spanish town.
   pueblo plaza mission

CHECK YOUR FACTS

4. In what year was Los Angeles founded?
5. What buildings were built around plazas?
6. What American Indian people lived in Los Angeles when the Spanish came?

THINK ABOUT IT

People of Spanish background are often called Hispanics (his SPAN iks). Do any Hispanic-Americans live in your community? Do you know their names?

Lesson 2: Rancho Days

NEW WORDS

rancho
fiesta

Los Angeles first belonged to Spain, a nation in Europe. Thirty years after the town was founded, Mexico won a war with Spain. Mexico then became an independent nation. Los Angeles was part of this new nation.

Around that time, raising cattle became important in Los Angeles. Cows and bulls were used for meat. Their skins were dried and used for leather. Leather was used to make many things then, just as it is today.

Skins from cattle could also be traded. They were traded for forks and spoons, tables, and beds. They were traded for suits, silk, earrings, and shoes. All these things were brought in ships to Los Angeles.

To raise cattle, a lot of grassy land was needed. There was much unused land around Los Angeles in those days. The Mexican government gave pieces of land to soldiers and important government workers. On the land they built ranchos.

Ranchos were like small communities. The family that owned a rancho lived in the main house. Sometimes, aunts, uncles, and cousins lived with them. The servants, cowhands, and field workers were usually American Indians. They lived on the rancho, too, in small houses. Some ranchos had a place for drying cattle skins. Some had a shop where people built things out of wood. Many had a small church. Some even had a jail. There were as many as 70 ranchos around El Pueblo de Los Angeles.

Life at a rancho was lively. The cowhands had many ways of having fun. They had bullfights and rodeos. Dancing was also a big part of rancho life, especially at **fiestas** (fee EHSS tuz), or holidays.

Cowhands herd cattle.

Horses help cowhands hold down a steer.

Owners of ranchos would ride into town to do business. Their families came to shop. They came to buy the nice things made in Europe. They also came in for big holidays like Christmas. Some families even had an extra house in town. Weddings were held in the town church.

Rancho days did not last. In 1848, the United States won a war against Mexico. California became a part of the United States. New settlers began to come to California. They wanted land. So the rancho lands were broken up and sold.

REVIEW

CHECK YOUR FACTS

1. Los Angeles has been part of three different nations. Name them.
2. List three ways in which cattle were used in the early days.
3. What people were given land to build ranchos?
4. Name the people who lived on a rancho.
5. Why were rancho lands broken up and sold?

THINK ABOUT IT

Do any communities in your state have Spanish names? If not, can you name any in other states?

A wagon train crosses the desert.

Lesson 3: Los Angeles Grows

Los Angeles was started by 46 people. By 1900, there were more than 100,000 people. Why did so many people move to Los Angeles?

Many arrived after 1848. In that year, California became part of the United States. At first, the new settlers came slowly. It was hard to get to Los Angeles. Wagon trains had to cross wide plains, mountains, and deserts. Other people came by sea. Both ways took a long time. Both were dangerous.

In 1848, gold was discovered in California. Many people came looking for gold. Others came to farm. The soil was good. There was lots of sun. Soon, oranges, potatoes, and wheat were growing all around Los Angeles.

In 1876, the Pacific Railroad reached Los Angeles. The Pacific Railroad connected with other railroads that crossed the whole nation. Now, it was easier to get to and from Los Angeles.

Los Angeles grew into a city.

By 1900, Los Angeles looked different. Buildings were made out of wood, brick, or stone. They had plumbing. Many buildings were several stories high. The streets were paved. Trolley cars took people from one end of the town to the other. Los Angeles was not a pueblo anymore. It was becoming a city.

REVIEW

CHECK YOUR FACTS

1. In 1900, Los Angeles had (more/fewer) than 100,000 people.
2. What important discovery was made in California in 1848?
3. What made it easier for people to get to Los Angeles?
4. By 1900, Los Angeles (was/was not) still a pueblo.

THINK ABOUT IT

Look at the picture of Los Angeles on this page. How do you think the streets and buildings changed from the time when Los Angeles was founded?

Lesson 4: Resources and Industries

NEW WORD
aqueduct

Two resources that brought people to Los Angeles were the farmland and the warm weather. As the city grew, another resource became very important. That was water. At first, the people got most of their water from the Los Angeles River. Some people also dug wells. But there was still not enough water.

Then William Mulholland had an idea. He thought of a way to bring more water into Los Angeles. There was water in the Owens River hundreds of miles away. The river was northeast of Los Angeles in the Sierra Nevada. The water would have to be brought across dry land. An aqueduct from the Owens River to Los Angeles might do it. An **aqueduct** is a waterway made of pipes, tunnels, and canals. It carries water from one place to another.

Mulholland convinced the people of Los Angeles that his plan would work. In 1907, work on the aqueduct began. Six years later, it was finished. Now the city had plenty of water. Later, Los Angeles got water from other places.

In 1892, Los Angeles discovered it had another important resource. In that year, Edward Doheny drilled a well for water on his land. Instead, he found petroleum. This started a big petroleum business in the Los Angeles area. People drilled oil wells in their backyards. They tore down their houses to make room for more wells. Years later, more petroleum was found.

Actors rest between shots.

Oil wells are higher than the trees in this old picture of Los Angeles.

Los Angeles was a good place in which to make movies. It had good weather all year. Movies could be made outdoors. There were different kinds of settings nearby. There were green woods, deserts, mountains, and flat land. The Hollywood area of Los Angeles became the main center of the movie business. Today, many TV shows are also made in Los Angeles.

The growing airplane companies also came to Los Angeles. During the 1920s, several airplane factories were built. These factories grew larger over the years. Los Angeles still has many jobs for workers making airplanes.

REVIEW

CHECK YOUR FACTS

1. At first, what two important resources brought people to Los Angeles?
2. What resource became an important need as the city grew?
3. What important resource was discovered in 1892?
4. What important business is in the Hollywood area of Los Angeles?
5. What kind of factories were built in Los Angeles in the 1920s?

THINK ABOUT IT

Could Los Angeles have grown so big if more water had not been brought in? Could many people live where there is little water?

Lesson 5: New People

NEW WORD

barrio

Before 1900, most people in Los Angeles were White Americans from other states. There were not many Mexicans or Blacks. This was true even though Mexicans and Blacks were among the first people to settle Los Angeles.

Between 1850 and 1882, many Chinese came to California. They worked in the mines. They worked on farms and in factories. Many Chinese also helped build the railroads in California. Most Chinese settled in San Francisco. There, they started their own community within the city. This famous community is known as Chinatown. Some Chinese also settled in Los Angeles.

Around 1900, some Japanese came to live in Los Angeles. They, too, worked in mines and in

Left: Chinese and Mexicans settled in Los Angeles. *Right:* The streets of Little Tokyo are busy.

factories. Many worked on farms. Some got farms of their own. At one time, Japanese farmers grew a large part of the vegetables in California. They were the first people to make rice grow in California. Many Japanese lived in an area of Los Angeles called Little Tokyo. Tokyo is the capital of Japan.

From 1941 to 1945, the United States and Japan were at war. Japanese-Americans were put into work camps. They could not take care of their farms and homes. So many lost their property. This was a very sad time for Japanese-Americans.

After the war, the Japanese-Americans did not have farms to return to. They opened businesses. They became scientists and lawyers. They worked at many different jobs. Only a few were farmers. Most did not go back to live in Little Tokyo. They settled in many different parts of Los Angeles.

This Mexican-American works for the California Water System.

A large number of Mexicans came to Los Angeles between 1910 and 1930. They came to do farm work. But many moved to the city. In the city, they lived in neighborhoods called barrios. A **barrio** is a part of a city where most of the people speak Spanish. Many of the people in the barrios did not have good jobs at first.

Around 1930, many Black people came to Los Angeles. They came from cities in the East and from farmlands in the South. Most came to find jobs in the growing factories.

REVIEW

CHECK YOUR FACTS

1. What group made up most of the people in Los Angeles before 1900?
2. At first, where did the Japanese live in Los Angeles?
3. What happened to Japanese-Americans between 1941 and 1945?
4. What group came to Los Angeles between 1910 and 1930? What kind of work had they come to do?

THINK ABOUT IT

From what places did the people in your community come?

Lesson 6: Los Angeles Today

NEW WORD
pollution

Today, Los Angeles is the third-largest city in the United States. It is the second-largest urban area in our country.

Over the years, Los Angeles has been spreading out. The map on page 157 shows the Los Angeles area today. Note that there are many communities besides Los Angeles itself.

The city has also been using land in new ways. Much of the land is used for large roads called freeways. These freeways connect the many communities that are part of Los Angeles. The city has also grown taller. Office buildings, hotels, and stores are now many stories high. Public places, such as sports stadiums, are very large. They must be big enough to hold more and more people as the population grows.

Left: There are tall buildings in downtown Los Angeles.
Below: Freeways are the best way to get around in Los Angeles.

LOS ANGELES URBAN AREA

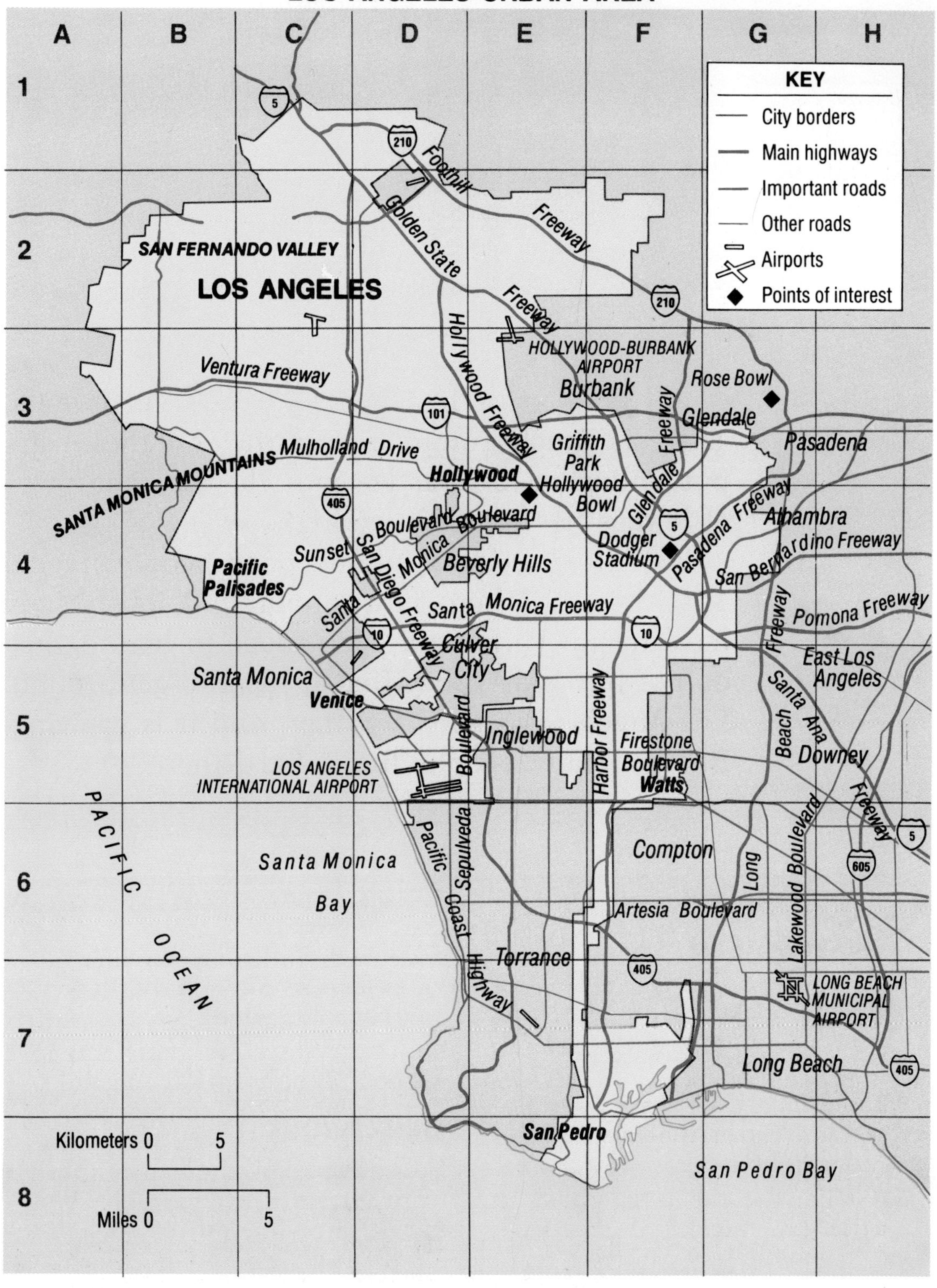

Cars fill the parking lot at a baseball game.

All this growth has also caused problems. There is much automobile traffic. All these cars put **pollution,** or wastes, into the air. The price of homes has gotten very high.

As in other cities, many poor people live in Los Angeles. Often they cannot find jobs. Many have trouble finding a good place to live. If they do not have cars, they find it hard to get around. Los Angeles has good weather, and it is growing. But for many people, life is hard there.

REVIEW

CHECK YOUR FACTS

1. How does Los Angeles rank in size among American cities?
2. There are (many/few) communities in the Los Angeles urban area.
3. What are the large roads in the Los Angeles area called?
4. Newer buildings in Los Angeles are often (taller/lower) than older ones.
5. There (are/are not) many poor people in Los Angeles.

THINK ABOUT IT

You have read about a number of problems a growing city can have. Name one other problem.

CHAPTER REVIEW

WATCH YOUR WORDS

1. ___were religious settlements.
   Pueblos Plazas Missions
2. The early Californians raised cattle on___.
   pueblos plazas ranchos
3. The early Californians celebrated holidays called___.
   fiestas barrios aqueducts
4. A(n) ___ carries water from one place to another.
   fiesta freeway aqueduct
5. Mexican neighborhoods in Los Angeles are called___.
   missions barrios ranchos

CHECK YOUR FACTS

6. What American Indian group lived in the Los Angeles area before outside settlers arrived?
7. Where did the group that started Los Angeles come from?
8. In what year did California become part of the United States?
9. What discovery in the year 1848 brought many people to California?
10. What resources did Los Angeles have plenty of? What resource did the city lack at first?
11. Name two kinds of businesses that became important in Los Angeles.
12. After the war, most Japanese (did/did not) go back to Little Tokyo.
13. What problems has growth caused in Los Angeles?

USE YOUR CHART AND MAP

14. Look at the time line for Los Angeles on page 145. When was the city founded?
15. What three resources are mentioned in the time line?
16. Look at the map of the Los Angeles area on page 157. How big is the city from north to south? From east to west?
17. Is the Los Angeles International Airport near or far from the ocean?

THINK ABOUT IT

18. What did Houston and Los Angeles have in common before they became part of the United States?
19. What resource has been important in both Houston and Los Angeles?
20. What might limit the growth of Los Angeles in the future?
21. What foreign language might you often hear spoken in Los Angeles?
22. Many sports teams have moved to the West. What examples can you think of?

CHAPTER 3 GOVERNING LOS ANGELES

Lesson 1: City Governments

NEW WORDS

- mayor
- city council
- district
- city manager

Like nations and states, all cities have governments. In our nation, there are two main kinds of city governments. One is called the mayor-council form of government. The other is the council-manager form of government. Most American cities have a mayor-council form of government.

Under the mayor-council form of government, the **mayor** is the leader of the city. The mayor heads the executive branch of the city government. The mayor is elected by all the people of the city. The mayor appoints the other members of the executive branch of the city government. In some cities, the mayor also appoints the judges of the city's courts.

The **city council** is the legislative branch of the city government. It makes the laws for the city. The members of the council are elected by the people in the city. In some cities, all the people vote for all the council members. In others, the city is divided into parts called **districts.** Then, the people in a district vote for only one council member.

Some cities have the council-manager form of city government. The council is elected by the people. The council then hires a **city manager** to run the city government. The city manager appoints the other members of the executive branch of the city government. Sometimes, there is also a mayor under this form of government.

This chart shows the two main kinds of city governments.

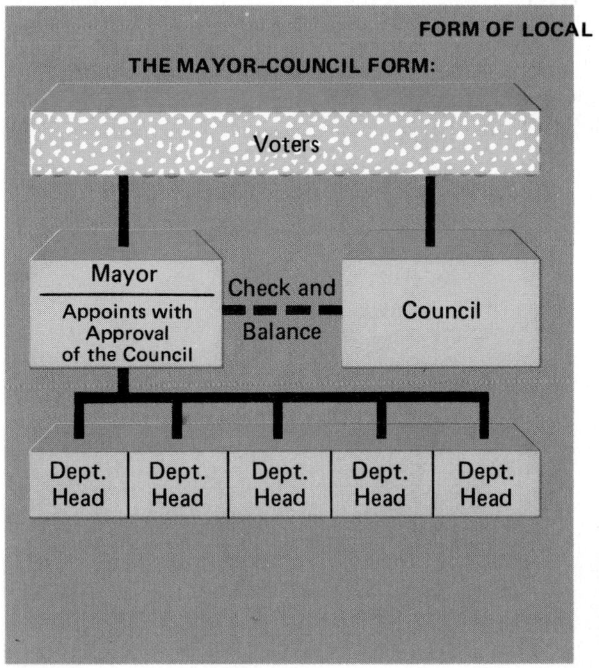

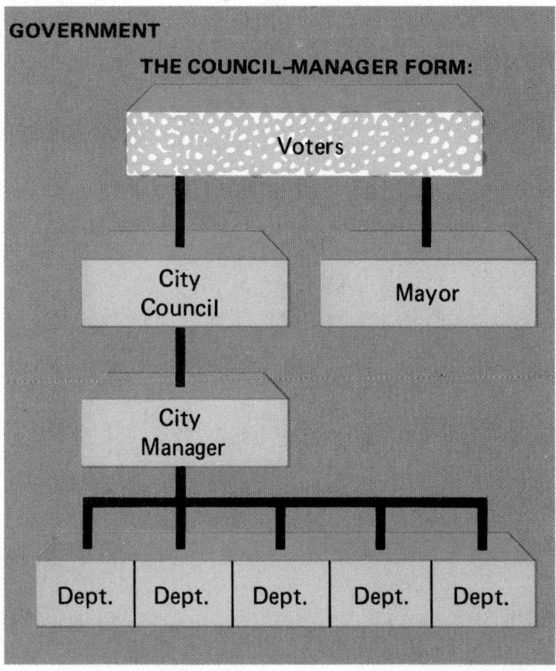

But, in that case, the mayor is only the head of the city council. He or she does not actually run the city government.

Each state decides what powers its cities will have. City governments are not even mentioned in the United States Constitution.

Most city governments furnish city services. They provide police, fire, and garbage services. They run city schools, libraries, and sometimes hospitals. They may be in charge of keeping the streets paved. They may provide water and sewers to carry off liquid wastes. Cities might also provide other services, such as housing for poor people. Usually, the bigger the city is, the more services it provides.

A woman speaks to a meeting of the city council.

FUN FACTS

Los Angeles is not the only interesting city in the West. Beautiful Seattle is the largest city in Washington. It lies on Puget Sound, which is connected to the Pacific. There are snow-covered mountains on two sides of the city.

Underneath the city is another Seattle. There was a fire in Seattle in 1889. Afterward, the level of the streets was raised. You can still walk the old streets and see the old stores. But now they are all underground!

A fire fighter comforts a child.

REVIEW

WATCH YOUR WORDS

1. Under the council-manager form of government, the ___ runs the city.
council mayor
city manager

2. The members of the city council are sometimes elected from___.
districts mayors
governments

CHECK YOUR FACTS

3. What form of government do most American cities have?

4. Council-manager governments (never/sometimes) have mayors.

5. Cities get their powers from (states/the Constitution).

THINK ABOUT IT

If you live in a city, find out what form of government it has.

Lesson 2: Government in Los Angeles

It takes many workers to run the city of Los Angeles. The city has thousands of police officers, fire fighters, and trash collectors. City workers build and fix city roads. They drive the city buses. They work in hospitals helping the sick. Libraries are also run by city workers. Hundreds of people take care of the city's parks and playgrounds. Others help the city's children in many ways. Some workers help collect taxes. These taxes help pay for the services the city provides to all its people.

Right: Government offices are in City Hall.

Below: Mayor Tom Bradley works at his desk.

City workers have leaders to help them make decisions. The police commissioner leads the police. The fire commissioner leads the fire fighters. Workers in other city departments have leaders, too.

Los Angeles has the mayor-council form of city government. The mayor is the leader of the whole city. Every 4 years, the people of Los Angeles choose a mayor. Mayor Tom Bradley used to be a police officer. Then, he ran for the job of mayor. In the first election, he lost. Then, 4 years later, he ran again and won.

Mayor Bradley decides what city problems need help first. He chooses commissioners and other department leaders. He picks the people he thinks will do a good job. They all work together to solve the problems of the city.

The city of Los Angeles is divided into 15 districts. The people in each district choose a council member. The council members help the mayor solve city problems.

Every weekday morning at 10 o'clock, the council meets at City Hall. The members talk about problems in each district.

The council makes laws and decisions for the city of Los Angeles. Mayor Bradley and the other city leaders see that the laws are carried out.

The mayor, the council, and the department leaders are important people. They help see that the city of Los Angeles runs well. Solving the problems of such a large city is a lot of work!

REVIEW

CHECK YOUR FACTS

1. It takes (many/few) workers to run Los Angeles.
2. Who helps city workers make decisions?
3. Who leads the whole city?
4. Into what parts is Los Angeles divided?
5. What group of leaders makes laws for Los Angeles?
6. Where does this group meet?

THINK ABOUT IT

Find out the name of the leader of your community.

CHAPTER REVIEW

WATCH YOUR WORDS

1. The ___ is the leader of the whole city.
   city manager council mayor
2. The ___ is hired by the council.
   city manager district mayor
3. Some cities are divided into ___.
   governments councils districts
4. The ___ is the legislative branch of city government.
   manager council district

CHECK YOUR FACTS

5. Name the two main forms of city government in the United States.
6. Cities (are/are not) mentioned in the Constitution of the United States.
7. Name some services that cities provide.
8. Larger cities tend to provide (more/fewer) services.
9. How often do the people of Los Angeles elect a mayor?
10. What does the council do for Los Angeles?

TRY SOMETHING NEW

11. Make a chart that shows the parts of the mayor-council form of city government.
12. Make a chart that shows the parts of the council-manager form of city government.
13. Write an advertisement for the job of manager in your city or one nearby. Stress the good things about the city.
14. Make a chart about city services. List some kinds of city workers. Beside each kind, write the duties that worker performs.

CHAPTER 4 AN ISLAND CITY

Lesson 1: A Vacation Paradise

Imagine a city on an island far out in the ocean. The island has beautiful beaches and tall mountains. It has palm trees and colorful flowers. A gentle wind blows from the northeast. The weather is never too hot. It is never too cold. It rains for only a few hours at a time.

The people who live on this island came from many lands. They have different ways of living. They eat different foods and wear different clothing. Yet, the different groups get along very well.

This city is Honolulu. The island is named Oahu (oh AH hoo). It is one of a group of 132 islands far out in the Pacific Ocean. These islands make up the State of Hawaii. Hawaii is the only state not on the mainland of the continent of North America. It was also the last state to enter the union. Hawaii became a state in 1959.

Each year, about 4 million people visit Hawaii. Many go for a vacation. They go for the beautiful sights, the beaches, and the weather. They go also for the warm welcome that Hawaiians give them.

Honolulu is the capital of Hawaii. It is the only American city that was once the capital of an independent kingdom. About 365,000 people live in Honolulu. It is by far the largest city in Hawaii and the only urban area. The city is important for the armed forces of the United States.

REVIEW

CHECK YOUR FACTS

1. The people of Hawaii came from (many/few) lands.
2. What island is Honolulu on?
3. In what ocean are the Hawaiian Islands?
4. When did Hawaii become a state?
5. Hawaii has (many/few) visitors each year.

THINK ABOUT IT

Bodies of water keep weather from getting as hot or cold as it otherwise might. How does this explain the weather in Hawaii?

Lesson 2: The History of Hawaii

Around the year 1200, a large group of people left home in big canoes. A **canoe** is a long, light, narrow boat. These people were Polynesians. They lived on islands in the Pacific Ocean. The Polynesians had heard of other islands across the sea. They wanted to live there. After a time, they found the Hawaiian Islands.

NEW WORDS

canoe
plantation
territory
citizen

In January 1778, James Cook, a British captain, stopped in Hawaii. He was the first known European visitor to the islands. After Cook came, traders began arriving in the islands.

In 1782, a war began among the people of the islands. It lasted for several years. At the end of the war, one chief, Kamehameha, became ruler. He became king of the Kingdom of Hawaii. By 1810, all the islands were under his rule.

During the 1800s, many American whaling ships stopped in Hawaii. There, they bought food and fresh water. The islands became a center of

Left: Liliuokalani was the last queen of Hawaii. *Right:* In 1816, Honolulu looked like this to a visitor from Europe.

Left: Hawaii grows lots of pineapples.
Top: Sugar cane is also an important crop in Hawaii.

trade in the Pacific. In 1835, Americans started the first sugar plantation. A **plantation** is a big farm. Pineapples later became a big crop.

Workers were needed on the plantations. But there were not enough Hawaiians to do the work. In the 1850s, Chinese began to arrive. In 1868, Japanese came. In the 1900s, Filipinos, Koreans, and Puerto Ricans began to come.

In 1891, Queen Liliuokalani (lee LEE oo oh kah LAH nee) became ruler of Hawaii. She tried to take more control of the government for the Hawaiian people. But the American planters were against this. In 1893, they took over the government. The following year, they set up the Republic of Hawaii. But they wanted the United States to take over the islands. In 1898, the American government took over Hawaii. In June 1900, the islands became a territory of the United States. A **territory** is an area with less power than a state. The Hawaiians became American citizens. A **citizen** is a member of a nation.

WHERE WE ARE IN TIME AND PLACE

TIME LINE FOR HAWAII

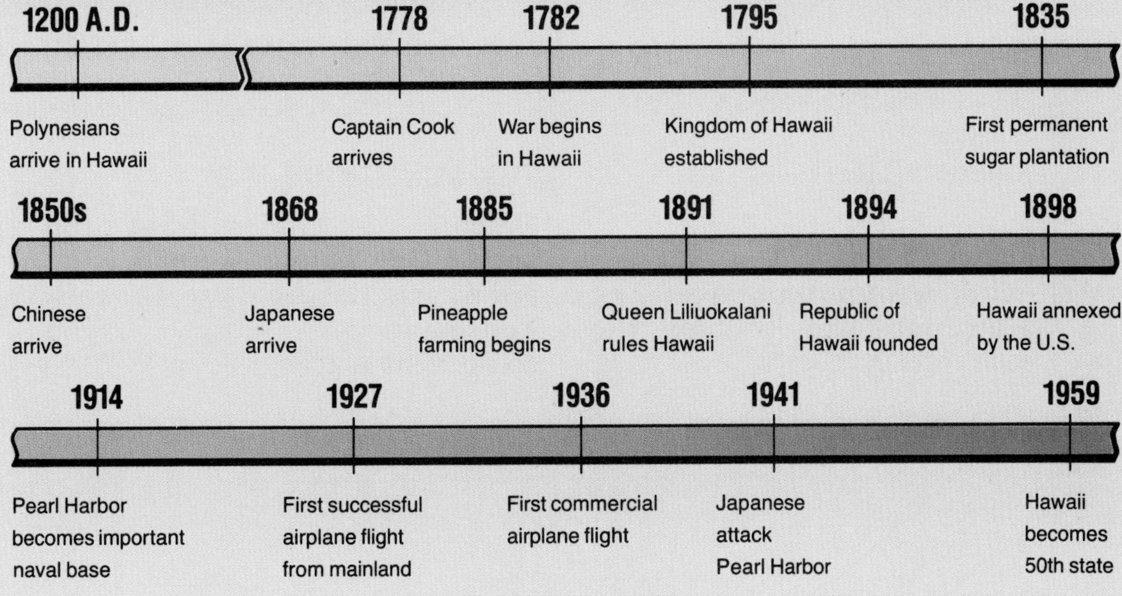

STATE OF HAWAII

PACIFIC OCEAN
Kauai
Niihau
Oahu
Kaneohe
Waipahu
Kailua
Pearl Harbor
Honolulu
Hawaiian Islands
Molokai
Maui
Lanai
Kahoolawe
Hawaii
Mauna Kea
Hilo
Mauna Loa
N
NE
E
SE
S
SW
W
NW

KEY
★ State capital
• Cities
Mountains

Kilometers 0 50 100 150
SCALE
Miles 0 50 100

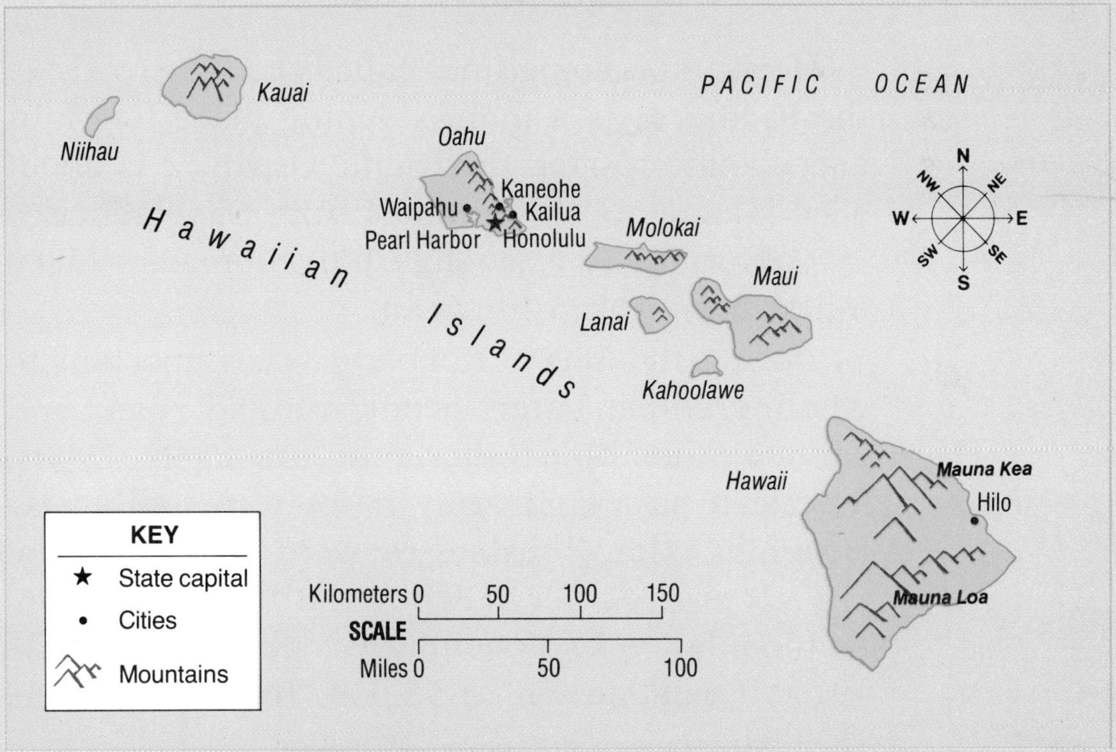

REVIEW

WATCH YOUR WORDS

1. A___is a large farm.
   territory canoe plantation
2. A ___ has less power than a state.
   kingdom territory citizen

CHECK YOUR FACTS

3. What group took over the Hawaiian Islands about the year 1200?
4. What European visited the islands in 1778?
5. When did Hawaii become an American territory?

TRY SOMETHING NEW

Hawaii is a wonderful vacation spot. Get some information about sightseeing in Hawaii. You could write letters. Or you could visit a travel agency.

Lesson 3: Honolulu Grows

NEW WORD

tourist

Honolulu is sometimes called the crossroads of the Pacific. It is a main stopping place for ships and planes crossing the Pacific Ocean. It is about 3860 kilometers (2400 miles) from San Francisco in California. It is about 6120 kilometers (3800 miles) from Tokyo in Japan.

During the 1800s, Honolulu was important to whaling ships. Later, people refined sugar and canned pineapples there. In the early 1900s, American navy and army bases were built near Honolulu. Many businesses were started in the city to provide services for the bases. In 1896, the population of Honolulu was about 30,000. By 1920, it had grown to 95,000. By 1930, it was 137,000.

In 1936, an event took place that was important for Honolulu. In that year, the first commercial planes began flying people to the islands. This made the trip much faster.

On December 7, 1941, Japanese planes bombed the navy base at Pearl Harbor, near Honolulu. They did much damage to the base. They sank many ships. As a result, the United States entered World War II against Japan. Honolulu became the main base for the American army and navy in the Pacific. The city became very crowded. In 1945, the United States won the war with Japan.

In 1950, Hawaii adopted a new constitution. It was to become law when Hawaii became a state. But some people in Congress were afraid to let Hawaii become a state. They feared that

Waikiki Beach is a popular place.

Japanese bombs sink a battleship at Pearl Harbor.

the Hawaiian people would not support the United States in another war. However, Hawaii finally became a state in 1959.

Honolulu grew slowly until the 1960s and 1970s. By then, fast, cheap air transportation brought many tourists to the islands. **Tourists** are people visiting a place on vacation. Many tall hotels and apartment houses were built. Waikiki (WY kee KEE) Beach became the center of the tourist business. Soon, tourists were a very important source of income in Honolulu. Only the navy and army spent more money there.

Honolulu is still booming. But growth has begun to cause problems. In some parts of Honolulu, there is much traffic and crowding.

Some people are afraid that Honolulu will be ruined by too many buildings. Because of this fear, building is not allowed in some places around Honolulu. One such place is Diamond Head. This is a small mountain near the city.

The most interesting thing about Hawaii is its people. Hawaii is the only state in which most people do not have a European background.

REVIEW

CHECK YOUR FACTS

1. Why is Honolulu sometimes called the crossroads of the Pacific?
2. American Navy and army bases (are/are not) important to Honolulu.
3. What important event took place near Honolulu in 1941?
4. Today, tourists (are/are not) important to Hawaii.
5. In Hawaii, most people (do/do not) have a European background.

THINK ABOUT IT

What place in or near Honolulu would you most like to visit? Why?

Lesson 4: The People of Honolulu

NEW WORDS

- custom
- aloha
- hula
- luau
- lei
- ukulele

In most American cities, only a small part of the population is of Asian background. But Honolulu is different. Look at the chart on page 177. Note that Japanese-, Chinese-, Hawaiian-, and Filipino-Americans make up more than half the population.

The people of Honolulu are very proud of their city. They know it is a true melting pot of people from many lands. Each group has given something to the city's way of life.

The first Hawaiians had many interesting **customs,** or ways of doing things. Many of these customs are still part of life in Hawaii. Almost everyone in Hawaii speaks English. But the people use many Hawaiian words as well. The words listed here are Hawaiian words. You may already know some of them.

aloha	ah LOH hah	welcome, goodbye
hula	HOO luh	a dance
luau	LOO ow	a feast
lei	LAY	a wreath of flowers

Hawaiian children dance and wear leis for a holiday.

A Hawaiian woman makes leis.

Hawaiians wear colorful clothes. Shirts and dresses usually have bright flowers on them. People sometimes wear leis, or flowers strung together. At luaus, or big feasts, people may dance the hula. Hula dances tell stories to music. Hawaiians developed the **ukulele** (YOO kuh LAY lee), a small guitar, and the Hawaiian steel guitar. *Ukulele* means "jumping flea." Throughout the year, there are special holiday celebrations that tourists go to. Hawaiians also like these special days.

Before World War II, some people in Hawaii did not trust Asian-Americans. They were afraid

ETHNIC GROUPS IN HONOLULU

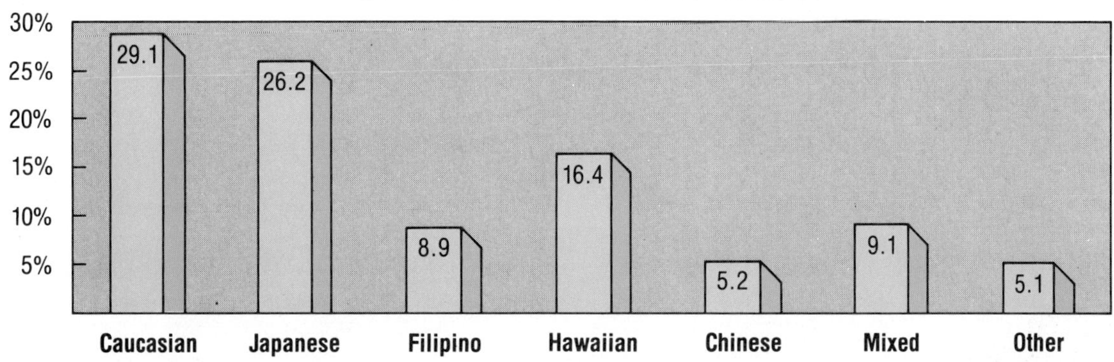

Asian-Americans would not be loyal to the United States during war. But these fears were proved wrong during World War II. There was not one case in Hawaii of an Asian-American not being loyal. Many Asian-Americans fought and died for the United States around the world.

After the war, Asian-Americans gained more respect in Hawaii. Some ran for public office. Japanese- and Chinese-Americans have been elected to many government jobs in Hawaii and Honolulu. For example, Hawaii's two United States senators are Japanese-Americans. They are Senators Daniel K. Inouye and Spark M. Matsunaga. Governor George R. Ariyoshi is Japanese-American, too. Asian-Americans have become active in almost all of Hawaii's businesses.

The future for Honolulu and its people is bright.

REVIEW

WATCH YOUR WORDS

1. ___are ways of doing things.
   Alohas Customs Hulas
2. ___means welcome.
   Aloha Lei Luau

CHECK YOUR FACTS

3. In most American cities, there are (many/few) Asians.
4. Name some Asian groups that are important to Hawaii.
5. Most Hawaiians (do/do not) speak English.

THINK ABOUT IT

Do any Asian-Americans live in your community? If so, from what parts of Asia did their families originally come?

CHAPTER REVIEW

WATCH YOUR WORDS

1. A___is a large farm.
plantation territory luau
2. A(n)___is a boat.
canoe aloha ukulele
3. A___is a member of a nation.
tourist lei citizen
4. Before Hawaii became a state, it was a___.
lei territory luau
5. A___is a small guitar.
luau ukulele aloha

CHECK YOUR FACTS

6. Honolulu is on what island?
7. Name two plantation crops that are important in Hawaii.
8. Who was Kamehameha?
9. What three groups arrived in Hawaii during the 1800s?
10. Who was Liliuokalani?
11. Is Honolulu closer to San Francisco or Tokyo?
12. Why was the beginning of commercial airplane flights important to Hawaii?
13. Today, the people of Hawaii (do/do not) use many Hawaiian words.
14. The Asian-Americans of Hawaii (have/have not) fought in wars for the United States.
15. Asian-Americans (have/have not) become government leaders in Hawaii.

USE YOUR CHART AND GRAPH

16. Look at the time line for Hawaii on page 170. Which plantation crop came first, sugar or pineapples?
17. About how long did the Kingdom of Hawaii last?
18. Look at the bar graph of Honolulu's population on page 177. What is the largest single group of people?
19. What is the second-largest group in Honolulu?
20. About how many people out of 100 in Honolulu are of Hawaiian background?

THINK ABOUT IT

21. Do you think Hawaii would have become a state without the airplane? Why, or why not?
22. In what ways is the beauty of Hawaii a problem?
23. Why are the original Hawaiians no longer the largest group in Honolulu?
24. Can you name any other Hawaiian Islands besides Oahu?
25. Hawaii was the last state to enter the Union. Is there any other area you think might become a state someday? What is it?

UNIT REVIEW

WATCH YOUR WORDS

Use the words to fill in the blanks. Use each term only once.

aqueduct	islands	plaza
citizens	mayor	pueblos
city council	mestizos	ranchos
customs	missions	seacoast
deserts	natural environments	territory
districts	plantations	valley

Seacoasts, mountains, valleys, and deserts are ___ of the Western United States. In the ___, it rarely rains. California has a huge ___ between its mountain ranges. The area near the ocean, the ___, changes greatly from north to south. One state in the West, Hawaii, is a group of ___.

Most of the 46 people who founded Los Angeles were ___. They came from ___, which are towns in Mexico. They built a town around a square, or ___. Nearby, there were religious settlements called ___. There were also cattle-raising communities called ___. Life there was lively, especially at holidays. As Los Angeles grew, water had to be brought in with a(n) ___.

In Los Angeles today, the ___ is the leader of the whole city. The members of the ___ represent ___, or parts of the city.

Hawaii was once ruled by the Polynesians. But many Americans came to set up sugar and pineapple ___. In 1900, Hawaii became a United States ___. That made the Hawaiians American ___. Today, many old Hawaiian ___ survive.

CHECK YOUR FACTS

1. The Western United States lies between what two things?
2. What area lies between the Sierra Nevada and the Rocky Mountains?
3. In California, redwood trees grow in the (north/south).
4. California (does/does not) have large urban areas.
5. Where did the first settlers of Los Angeles come from?
6. What was raised on ranchos?
7. When was gold discovered in California?
8. Why did Los Angeles have to build an aqueduct?
9. What business is centered in Hollywood, California?

10. What group played a large part in building the railroads in California?

11. What group settled in the Little Tokyo area of Los Angeles?

12. How are the communities of Los Angeles connected with one another?

13. Name the two main kinds of city government.

14. What form of government does Los Angeles have?

15. What state of the United States is not on the mainland of North America?

16. What is the name of the largest city in Hawaii?

17. Why did people come from Asia to work on Hawaii's sugar plantations?

18. What city is sometimes called the crossroads of the Pacific?

19. What nation attacked Hawaii in 1941?

CLOSE THE MAP GAP

20. Draw a map of the Western United States. Show and label the states and their capitals. Also label Canada, Mexico, the Rocky Mountains, and the Pacific Ocean.

21. Draw a map of California. Show and label the Pacific Ocean, the Coast Ranges, the Central Valley, the Sierra Nevada, and the Mojave Desert.

USE YOUR MAPS

22. Look at the map of the Western United States on page 136. List the rivers shown.

23. What is the capital of Alaska?

24. Look at the map of California's natural environments on page 138. What important city is located in the Central Valley?

25. Look at the map of Los Angeles on page 157. What important community that is *not* part of Los Angeles is located in squares *D4* and *E4*?

THINK ABOUT IT

26. How has weather been important in the history of Los Angeles and Honolulu?

27. Do you think many or few people tend to live in deserts? Give reasons for your answer.

TRY SOMETHING NEW

28. By writing letters, or in other ways, get tourist information on Los Angeles or Honolulu.

PUT IT ALL TOGETHER

29. Make a chart that shows what Los Angeles and Honolulu are like. Include things like weather, location, and businesses. Also include groups of people and number of people.

OUR NORTHERN NEIGHBOR

UNIT 4

CHAPTER 1 THE NATION OF CANADA

Lesson 1: Canada Is Our Neighbor

NEW WORD

province

The United States and Canada share a large part of the continent of North America. Find these two countries on the map on page 185. Both are nations. Every nation has its own land, people, and government.

Study the map. Notice that most of Canada is north of the United States. It is closer to the North Pole. This means that the weather is very cold in parts of Canada during the winter. It is colder than in most parts of the United States except Alaska.

Canada
AHEAD 2 MILES
EN AVANT 2 MILLES

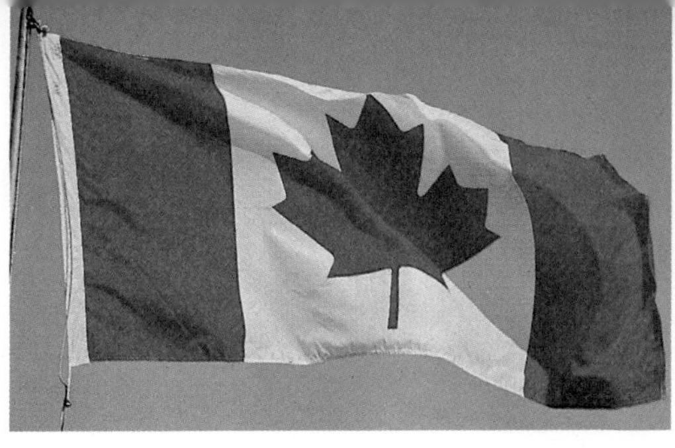

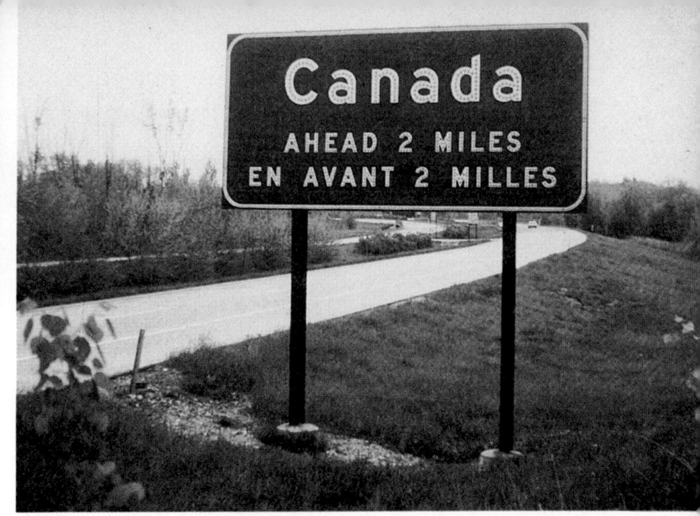

Top: The Canadian flag has a maple leaf in the middle.
Right: Canadians speak two languages, English and French.

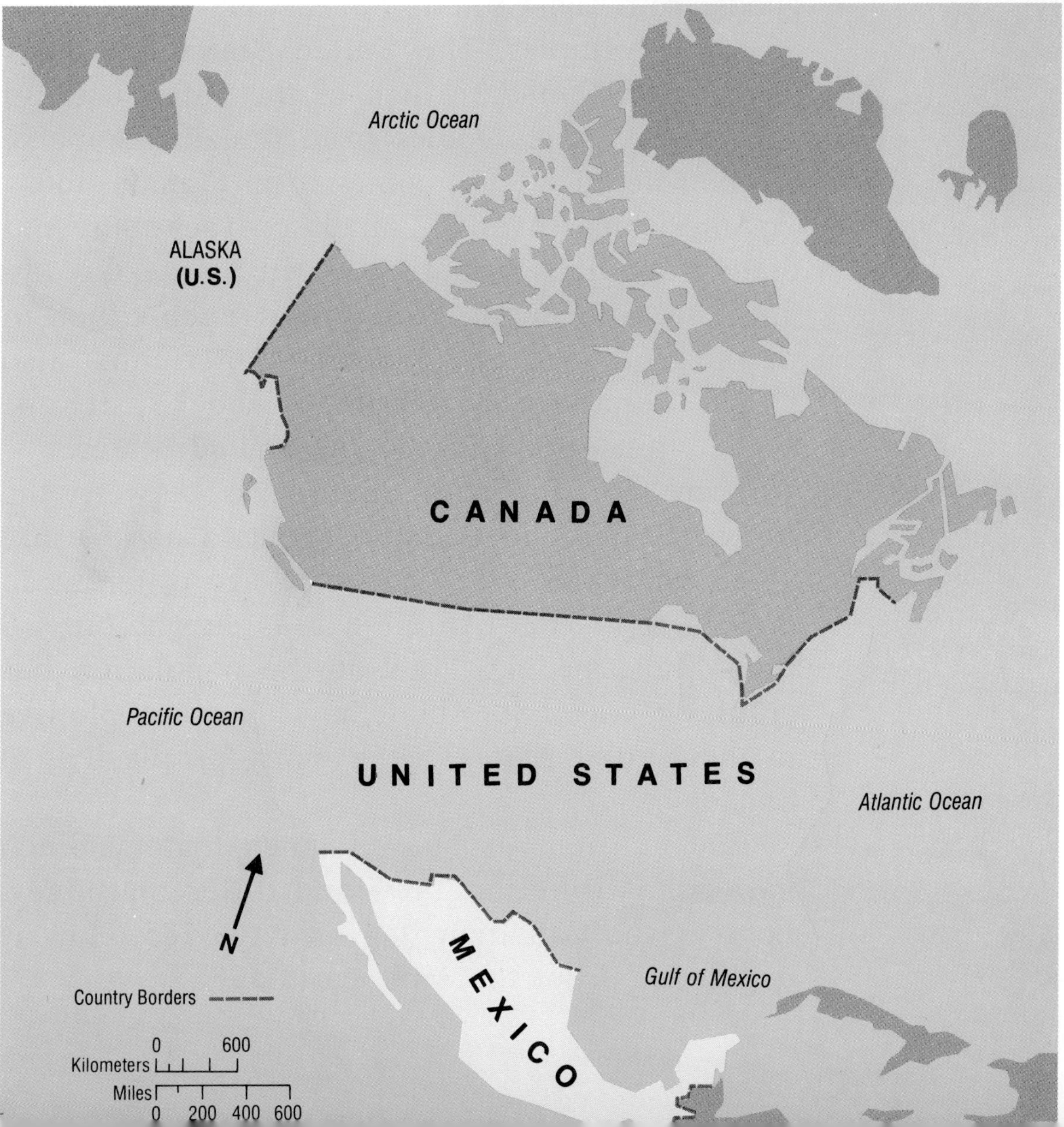
Arctic Ocean
ALASKA
(U.S.)
CANADA
Pacific Ocean
UNITED STATES
Atlantic Ocean
N
MEXICO
Gulf of Mexico
Country Borders
0
600
Kilometers
Miles
0 200 400 600

Most nations are divided into smaller parts. In the United States, the smaller parts are called states. In Canada, there are 10 smaller parts called **provinces.** There are also 2 territories in Canada.

Canada and the United States are neighbor nations. They share a long border.

These two nations also share in other ways. They are trading partners. Canada buys many goods from the United States. Cars and clothes are two examples. The United States also buys goods from Canada. Much of the paper used in the United States comes from Canada. Some of the petroleum we use comes from Canada, too.

Americans travel to Canada on vacations. And many Canadians visit the United States. Canadians and Americans read about each other in newspapers and magazines. Americans also watch Canadian baseball and hockey teams. These teams often play in the United States.

There are important differences between the United States and Canada. The two nations are about the same size. But they are different in population. The United States has about 10 times more people. Look at the population bar graph on page 188. About how many people live in the United States? How many people live in Canada?

Each nation also has its own history. Each nation has different laws and different money. Look at the Canadian flag on page 185. How is it different from the American flag?

WHERE WE ARE IN TIME AND PLACE

THE GROWTH OF CANADA

1867	1870	1871	1873	1905	1949
Quebec, Ontario, Nova Scotia, and New Brunswick set up Dominion of Canada	Province of Manitoba set up	British Columbia joins Canada	Prince Edward Island joins Canada	Alberta and Saskatchewan become provinces	Newfoundland joins Canada

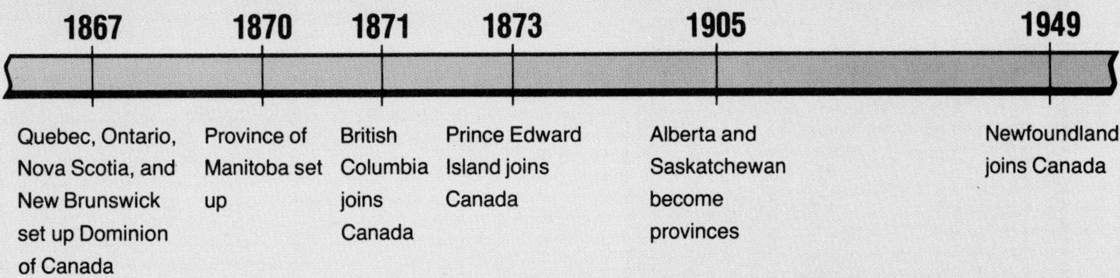

PROVINCES AND TERRITORIES OF CANADA

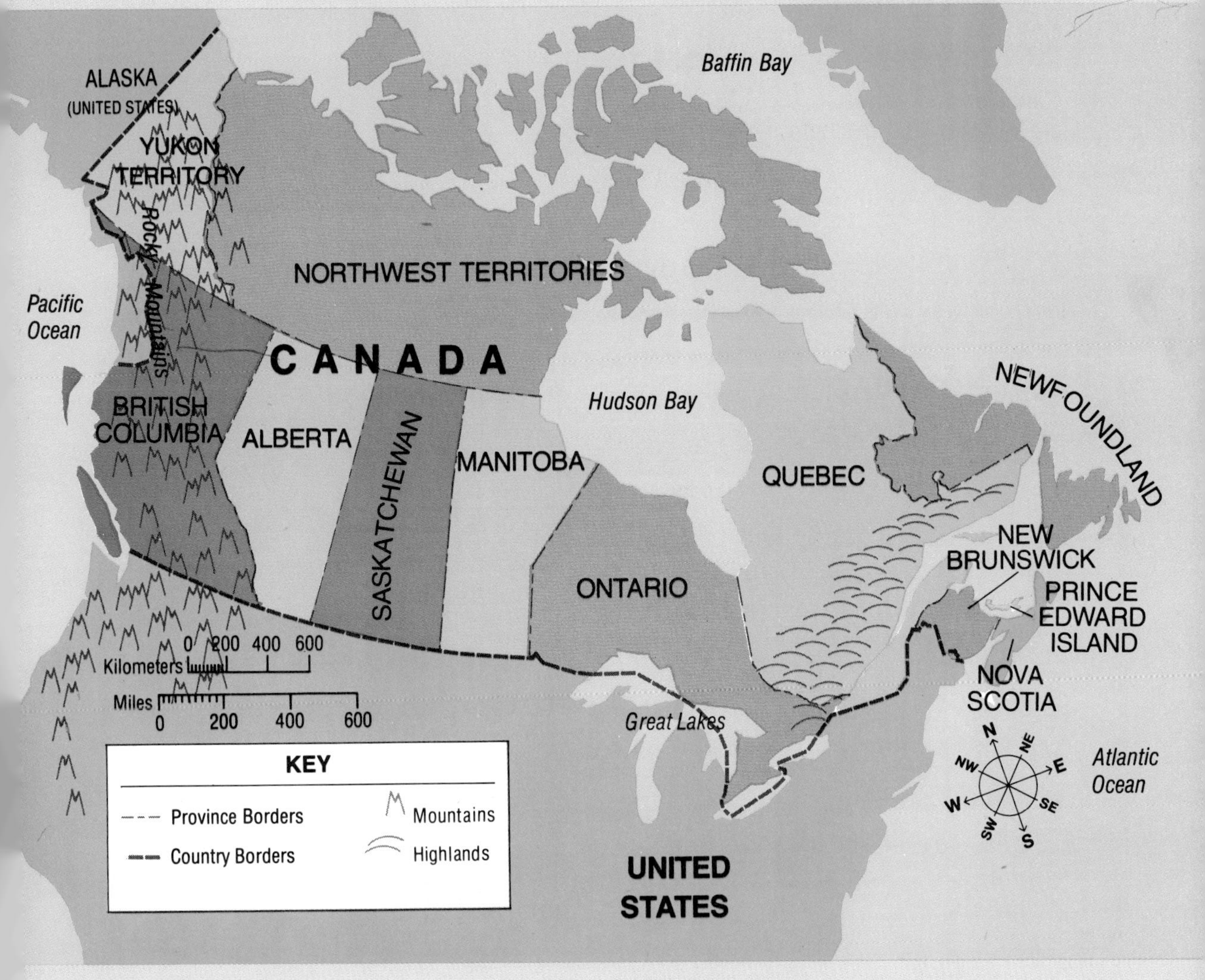

ALASKA
(UNITED STATES)
YUKON TERRITORY
Rocky Mountains
Pacific Ocean
NORTHWEST TERRITORIES
Baffin Bay
CANADA
BRITISH COLUMBIA
ALBERTA
SASKATCHEWAN
MANITOBA
Hudson Bay
QUEBEC
NEWFOUNDLAND
ONTARIO
NEW BRUNSWICK
PRINCE EDWARD ISLAND
NOVA SCOTIA
Great Lakes
Atlantic Ocean
0 200 400 600
Kilometers
Miles
0 200 400 600
KEY
Province Borders
Country Borders
Mountains
Highlands
N NE E SE S SW W NW
UNITED STATES

Canadian magazines are in both English and French.

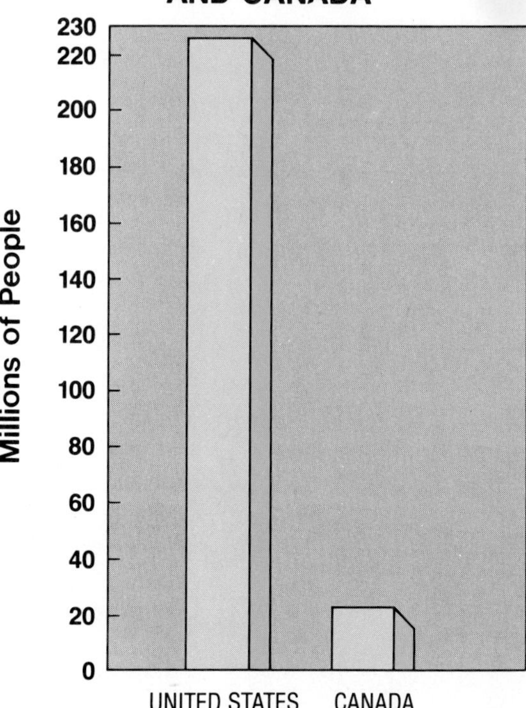

REVIEW

CHECK YOUR FACTS

1. Canada (does/does not) buy goods from the United States.
2. Name some goods the United States buys from Canada.
3. The United States and Canada (are/are not) about the same size.
4. The United States has (more/fewer) people than Canada.

LOOK AT THE MAP

5. There are several small provinces in (eastern/western) Canada.
6. What Canadian province borders on the Great Lakes?

LOOK AT THE LESSON

7. What three things does every nation have?
8. Most of Canada is (north/south) of the United States.
9. How many provinces are there in Canada?

TRY SOMETHING NEW

Draw and color a picture of the Canadian flag.

Lesson 2: The People of Canada

Long ago, only American Indians lived in Canada. They arrived thousands of years ago from Asia. Today, there are about 50 different American Indian groups.

Shoppers crowd a farmers' market.

The north of Canada is very cold. Even in summer, Innuit children wear sweaters. In winter, the Innuit dress for snow.

Young Canadians march and play music. Playing bagpipes and wearing plaid clothes are customs from Scotland.

The Eskimos, or Innuit (IN yoo it), came from Asia after the American Indians did. They have also been in Canada a long, long time. Most Innuit live in the north of Canada. It is very cold there.

European settlers started coming to Canada about 375 years ago. Most of these early settlers came from France. The French are still a large group in Canada today. They follow French customs. They speak the French language.

Later, most settlers came from England and Scotland. They spoke English. Today, more than half of all Canadians speak English. Canadians have also come from Germany and Italy. There are smaller groups from other places, too.

FUN FACTS

Today, Innuit use snowmobiles to get around. But some people in northern Canada still use the old way, dog sleds.

Eskimo dog is the name given to three kinds of dogs used to pull the sleds. Eskimo dogs carry their tails curled above their backs. This keeps the tail from dragging in the snow. This way, the dog's tail does not freeze. Eskimo dogs have thick fur that keeps them warm even in the coldest weather. Their large feet keep them from falling through the snow.

It takes at least three dogs to pull a sled. Some sleds need as many as eight dogs. The driver starts the dogs by yelling "Mush!" The front dog is called the lead dog. It takes the orders from the driver and shows the other dogs what to do.

A team of dogs can pull a sled 32 to 64 kilometers (20 to 40 miles) a day across the snow. Five dogs can pull a load of 113 kilograms (250 pounds).

You can see that different kinds of people are called Canadians. Many do not want to forget their own customs and languages. But they share a large country. They share a future in that country. They are all Canadians.

REVIEW

CHECK YOUR FACTS

1. What two groups came to Canada before the Europeans began to come?
2. Where did most of the first European settlers come from?
3. What language do more than half of the Canadians speak?
4. Name four countries in Europe from which Canadian settlers came.

THINK ABOUT IT

Everyone in Canada does not speak the same language. What problems can this cause?

CHAPTER REVIEW

CHECK YOUR FACTS

1. What continent is Canada on?
2. What part of the United States is north of much of Canada?
3. How many provinces and territories are there in Canada?
4. Name some goods Canada buys from the United States.
5. Canada has a (larger/smaller) population than the United States.
6. The money that is used in the United States and Canada is (the same/different).
7. Who were the first people to come to Canada?
8. What is another name for the Eskimos?
9. What was the first European group to come to Canada?
10. What two languages are important in Canada?

USE YOUR MAPS

11. Look at the map of North America on page 185. What three nations share most of the continent?
12. Look at the map of Canada on page 187. Name the Canadian territories.
13. Name the Canadian provinces and territory that border on the United States.
14. What Canadian province has a large area of highlands?
15. What Canadian province is an island?

THINK ABOUT IT

16. In the United States, 48 of the 50 states border on each other. Suppose you wanted to travel by land from one of these states to Alaska. What nation would you pass through?
17. Why is it important for the United States and Canada to be friends?
18. Many Canadians speak French. What foreign language do many Americans in New York, Florida, Texas, and the West speak?
19. Canada is a kingdom. Name the official ruler of Canada if you can.
20. Canadians have come to Canada from many lands. Is this also true of Americans in the United States?

CHAPTER 2 LOOKING AT CANADA

Lesson 1: Canada's Land

Imagine that you are traveling through the south of Canada. You are going from west to east. Before you start, look again at your map on page 187. Trace the route with your finger.

Here are some of the things you might see. British Columbia is on the Pacific Coast. Cities along the coast have harbors for ships. Farther inland, there are beautiful green forests.

The peaks of the Rocky Mountains rise along Alberta's border with British Columbia.

Grain fields and cattle ranches can be seen all over Saskatchewan (sas KACH uh WAHN) and Manitoba. There, the land is usually flat.

Ontario and Quebec are known for their good farmlands. They also have many rivers and

Vancouver, British Columbia, has a fine harbor.

lakes. Canada has more lakes than any other nation in the world.

The provinces of eastern Canada have coasts on the Atlantic Ocean. Small fishing villages can be found along their coasts.

REVIEW

CHECK YOUR FACTS

1. There (are/are not) important harbors on Canada's Pacific Coast.
2. What is on the border between British Columbia and Alberta?
3. What is most of the land like in the provinces of Saskatchewan and Manitoba?
4. What are Ontario and Quebec known for?
5. What can be found along the coasts of Canada's Atlantic provinces?

THINK ABOUT IT

Is the area where you live like any part of Canada? Which one? If your area is not like Canada, how is it different?

Lesson 2: Communities in Canada

Here are descriptions of some of Canada's well-known towns and cities. As you read, find these places on the map on page 199.

Below is Dawson, a small town in the Yukon Territory. Years ago, Dawson was an exciting place. In 1896, gold was found there. Thousands of people came to the Yukon Territory. They hoped to get rich. Today, most of the gold is gone from Dawson. Copper, lead, and silver are being mined instead.

Vancouver is a harbor city on the west coast. It is one of the largest cities in Canada. Big ships carry goods in and out of the city. Timber and fish are some of Vancouver's main resources.

Calgary lies in fine cattle country. Raising and selling cattle is a big business there. Oil and natural gas are important resources in Calgary.

Dawson is very far north.

Top left: Toronto has many new buildings. *Top right:* The government buildings in Ottawa are on the river. *Below left:* Calgary is a growing city. *Below right:* St. John's harbor is very busy.

The word *regina* (ri JY nuh) means "queen." Regina is the "Queen City of the Plains." This city is the capital of Saskatchewan. It was named in honor of Queen Victoria. She was queen of Great Britain in the 1800s. When the railroad reached Regina, the city became important to settlers. The Northwest Mounted Police made Regina their main office in 1882. Have you ever heard of the Canadian Mounties?

Winnipeg is the capital of Manitoba. This city was once a supply point for fur traders. Now, Winnipeg is a grain center of the world.

Toronto is the capital of Ontario. Although it is not on the ocean, Toronto is a port city. Can you tell from the map on page 199 how Toronto can be a port?

Every nation has a capital city. The capital is the city where the nation's government meets. The capital city of the United States is Washington, DC. The capital city of Canada is Ottawa. Ottawa has many large government buildings.

The city of St. John's is on the east coast of Newfoundland. Fishing boats and freighters use its harbor. St. John's has been an important fishing port for 300 years.

FUN FACTS

The Royal Canadian Mounted Police are the police force of Canada. The police became famous for two reasons. One was their colorful uniforms. The other was the quiet way they kept order in Canada's wild west.

In the old days, they rode horseback. Their full name then was the Northwest Mounted Police. But people called them "Mounties" for short. Mounties wore bright red jackets and wide-brimmed hats. The hats protected their heads from the hot sun of the plains.

Today, the Mounties ride horses only at special times. To get around most settled areas, they drive cars. But the Mounties also look after large areas of forests and lakes and the cold, snowy Canadian north. There, they use boats, helicopters, and snowmobiles to travel around.

Montreal is Canada's largest city. It is also Canada's main seaport. It has tall skyscrapers, new apartment buildings, and modern factories. There are some very old buildings there, too. You will learn more about Montreal later.

REVIEW

CHECK YOUR FACTS

1. Vancouver is on Canada's (east/west) coast.
2. Name two important resources of Calgary.
3. What does the name of the city of Regina mean?
4. What city is the capital of Canada?
5. What is Canada's largest city?

THINK ABOUT IT

Which Canadian city described in the lesson would you most like to visit? Why?

Lesson 3: Where Do Canadians Live?

Some parts of Canada have many people. Other parts have very few.

Look at the map on page 199. Dots show where most Canadians live. Each dot stands for 100,000 people. Many dots in an area mean that many people live there. One or two dots mean that fewer people live there. Areas that have no dots at all have a very small population.

Notice the blue line on the map. It shows the path of the Trans-Canada Highway. The highway

The Trans-Canada highway goes through the mountains.

goes across all of Canada from coast to coast. It connects most of the large Canadian cities.

Notice, too, that most dots are close to the Trans-Canada Highway. This highway is useful to most of Canada's people.

Use the scale on the map below to measure the following distances: from Ottawa to Winnipeg, from St. John's to Vancouver, from Dawson to Calgary.

POPULATION OF CANADA

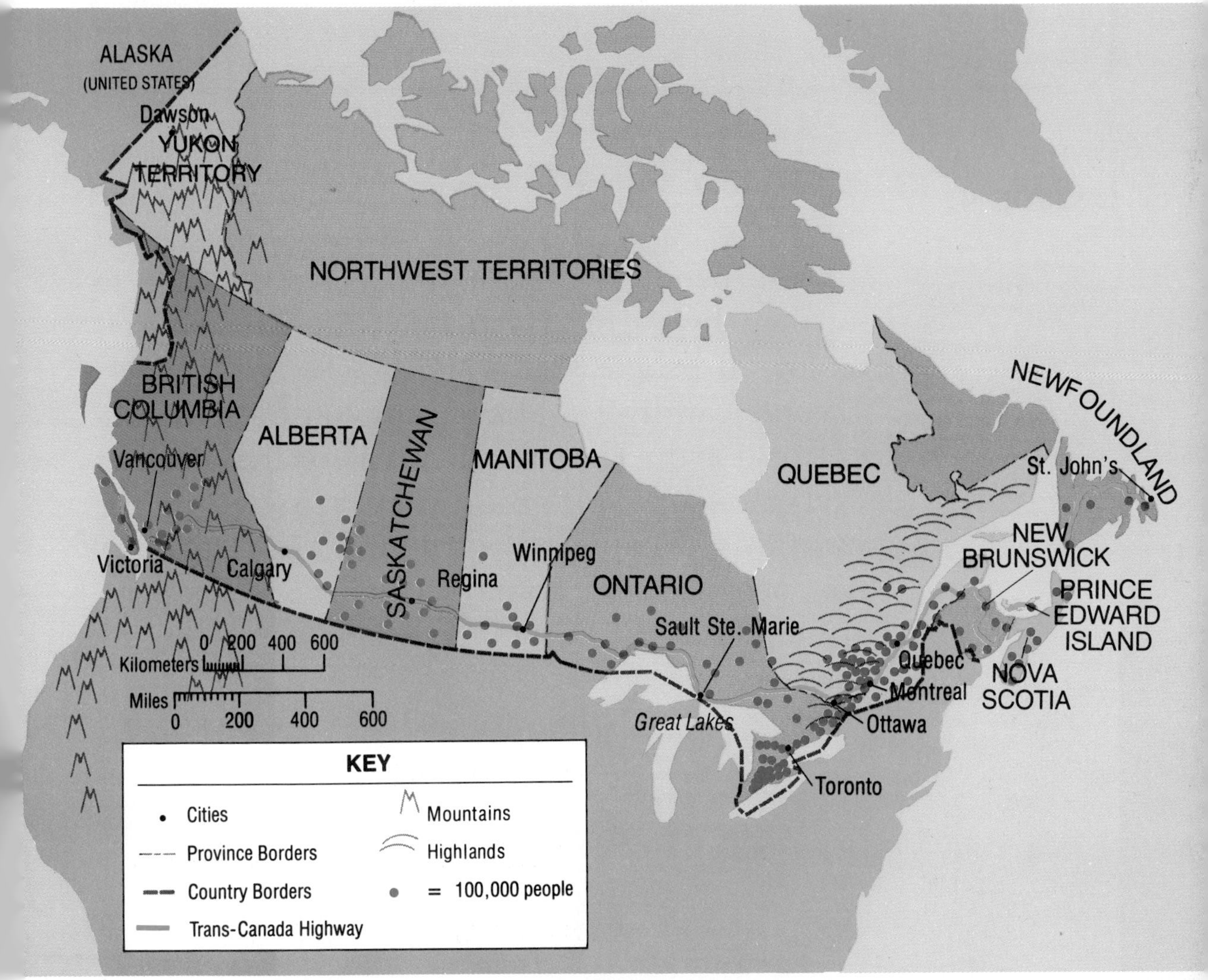

REVIEW

CHECK YOUR FACTS

Look at the Map

1. Are there more people in northern Canada or southern Canada?
2. What important city of eastern Canada does the Trans-Canada Highway not reach?

Look at the Lesson

3. Where does the Trans-Canada Highway go?
4. The Canadian people are spread (evenly/unevenly) across Canada.
5. Most Canadians live (near/far from) the Trans-Canada Highway.

THINK ABOUT IT

Why do you think people are spread across Canada in the way they are?

Lesson 4: People and the Environment

NEW WORDS

adapt
greenhouse

Where people live can make a difference in *how* they live. This is true for Canadians. It is true for all people.

People can live in almost any natural environment on Earth. They can live where the weather is very hot or very cold. They can live in the mountains or on very flat land. But, to stay alive, people must adapt to their environment. To **adapt** means to change when you need to.

Dogs pull a sled.

People who live in the desert learn how to save water. They must adapt in this way because they live in a very dry land.

Do you remember the town of Dawson in the Yukon Territory? Dawson has long and very cold winters. It snows about 150 centimeters (60 inches) every year. The short summers in Dawson are cool. How do you think people adapt to this environment?

The people of Dawson wear special clothes to keep out the cold. Their jackets and boots may be lined with fur. In winter, some people pack snow against the sides of their homes. This helps keep in the heat. It also protects against the wind. All homes have places to burn fuel for heat.

The people of Dawson travel in special ways. In winter, they use snowmobiles and sleds. For their food, they hunt in the forests of the Yukon. They fish in lakes and rivers. In spring, they are able to grow some vegetables in **greenhouses.** These buildings have glass walls that let the sun in. The walls also keep the cold out. So greenhouses stay very warm inside.

Other foods have to be brought into Dawson from other parts of Canada. First, ships bring the food to the coast. Then, the railroad takes the food to the town where the railroad ends. From there, the food is taken to Dawson by truck.

Now, find the city of Victoria on the map on page 199. Victoria is on an island off the southern part of British Columbia. The weather in Victoria is like spring. It is cool most of the time. It never gets too warm. Mild winds from the Pacific Ocean warm Victoria in winter. They cool it in summer. What kind of clothes do you think the people of Victoria wear?

The people of Victoria get much of their food nearby. The soil in the area is rich. Farmers raise dairy cattle and vegetables. There are many kinds of fish along the coast.

Look at the picture at the bottom of this page. How are the people in Victoria traveling? Of course, there are also cars and buses in Victoria. Transportation over water is very important, too.

Most of the people in British Columbia live in the southwest corner. Victoria is located there. Very few people live in the Yukon Territory. Only about 800 live in the town of Dawson. Can you explain why?

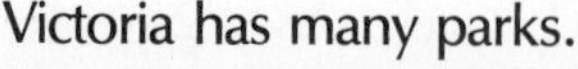
Victoria has many parks.

REVIEW

CHECK YOUR FACTS

1. People are able to live in (a few/many) kinds of natural environments.
2. What do people do to stay alive in their environment?
3. What are winters like in Dawson?
4. List four ways in which the people of Dawson get their food.
5. What is the weather in Victoria like?

THINK ABOUT IT

How have the people who live in your area adapted to their environment?

CHAPTER REVIEW

CHECK YOUR FACTS

1. What ocean does British Columbia border on?
2. What kinds of crops and animals are raised in Saskatchewan and Manitoba?
3. Ontario and Quebec (do/do not) have many rivers and lakes.
4. What discovery brought many people to the Yukon Territory?
5. For whom was the city of Regina named?
6. What city is the capital of Manitoba?
7. Toronto (is/is not) a port.
8. What important road crosses Canada?
9. Is the weather colder in Dawson or in Victoria?
10. What is the name of the capital city of Canada?

USE YOUR MAP

11. Look at the population map of Canada on page 199. Are there more people in eastern Canada or western Canada?
12. Does the Trans-Canada Highway cross all the Canadian provinces and territories?
13. About how far is it from Montreal to Toronto?

THINK ABOUT IT

14. Look at any of the maps of Canada. What is the name of the large island northeast of Canada?
15. What parts of Canada do you think are most like the United States?
16. Why do you think people live in cold places like Dawson?

CHAPTER 3 LEARNING ABOUT MONTREAL

Lesson 1: Looking at Montreal

The city of Montreal is in Quebec Province. Look at the map of Canada on page 187. Find the province of Quebec. Many French people came to Canada several hundred years ago. Most of them settled in Quebec.

The map on page 205 shows the central business district of Montreal. Notice that many of the names are not in English. They are in French. Most of the people in Montreal speak French.

Montreal is built on an island. The mighty St. Lawrence River flows along the east side of the city. This makes Montreal an important port. Ships sail between the Great Lakes and the Atlantic Ocean. They stop in Montreal. Many of the

MONTREAL CENTRAL BUSINESS DISTRICT

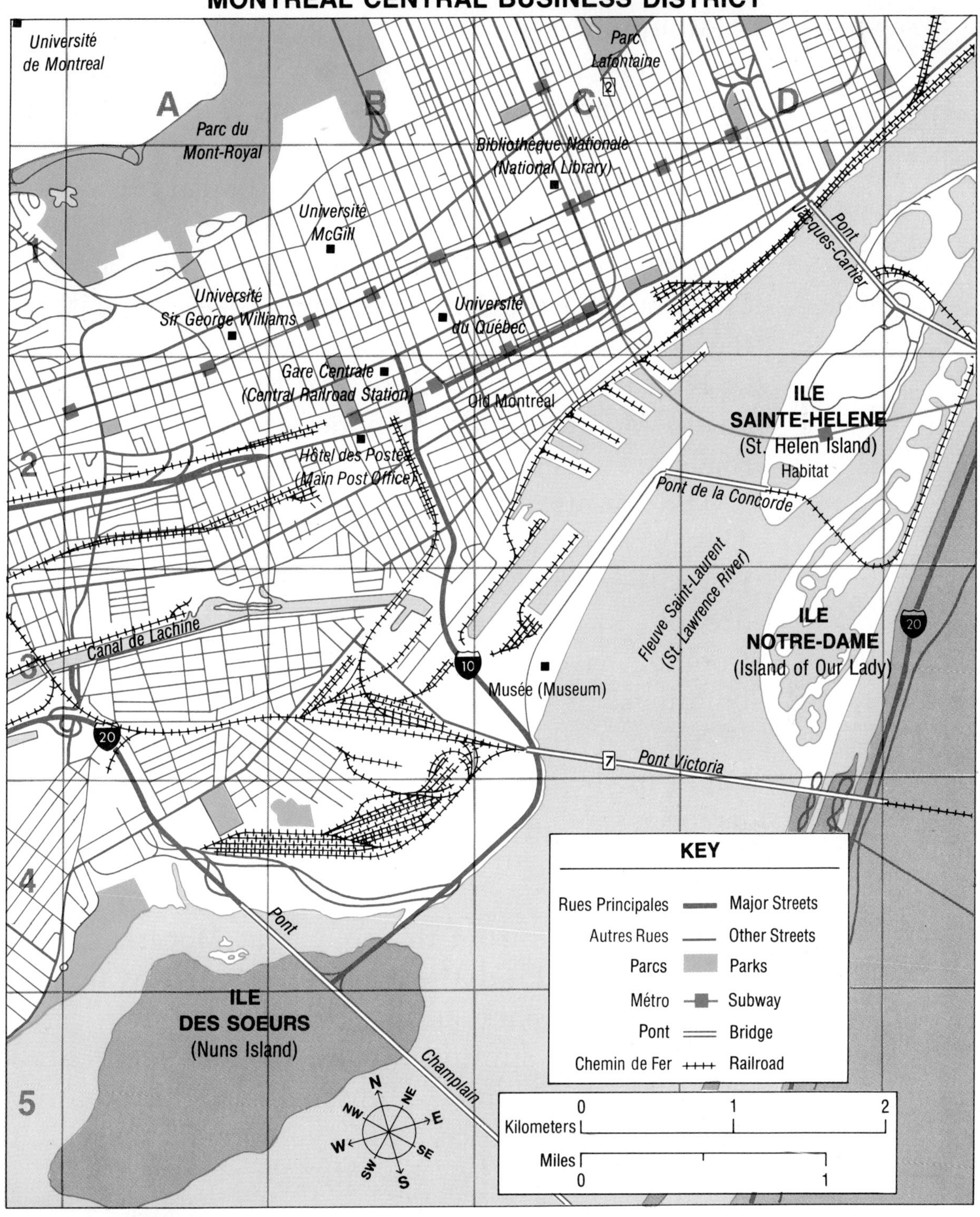

goods coming into or going out of Canada must pass through Montreal.

Montreal is an important transportation center. There are two important airports in the Montreal area. Railroads and highways connect Montreal with other large cities in Canada.

Look again at the map of the central business district of Montreal. Compare the central business district of Montreal with that of Kansas City on page 99. How are they alike? How are they different?

Find the docks for ships and the railroad lines on the Montreal map. Why do you think the railroads are so close to the waterfront?

Old Montreal is the oldest part of the city. This part of the city is also along the waterfront. Here, there are narrow, winding streets. There are old stone buildings and squares. Farther from the river are tall hotels, stores, and office buildings.

Some of the industrial areas in Montreal are found in the central business district. Montreal's factories prepare and package foods. They make clothes, cars, airplanes, medicines, and many other goods.

You can see from this map that Montreal has many parks. Find the Parc du Mont-Royal. In this beautiful park, people ride horse-drawn carriages in the summer. They ski and ice skate there in the winter. Montreal also has many other recreation areas. Hockey, football, baseball, golf, and boating are favorite sports.

REVIEW

CHECK YOUR FACTS

Look at the Maps

1. Near Montreal, there (are/are not) islands in the St. Lawrence River.
2. What canal is in the central business district of Montreal?

Look at the Lesson

3. On what river is Montreal?
4. What language do most of the people in Montreal speak?
5. Where is the section called Old Montreal located?

THINK ABOUT IT

Why are bridges important to Montreal?

Lesson 2: A Changing City

Montreal is a large city. It is still growing. As it grows, it changes.

In the last 40 years, there have been two main times of change.

Left: This old church is still in use. *Below:* Old houses are torn down.

The first began after World War II, around 1945. Many new people came to live in Montreal. Many of them had just moved to Canada. As the population grew, new problems had to be solved.

More people meant that more living spaces were needed. The city began to spread out. There were also more cars and more traffic. Old buildings were torn down. In their place, tall new buildings and parking lots were built. Some old and beautiful buildings were gone forever.

FUN FACTS

In crowded big cities, subway trains are the best way to get around. London, England, was the first city to build a subway. It was built in 1863. The London subway trains run in tunnels that are built deep below the ground. Some of the stations are so far down that passengers ride to the street in elevators.

Boston was the first city in the United States to build a subway. The first part of Boston's subway opened in 1897. New York opened a subway soon after that. New York subways grew with the city. Today, the New York subway system is the largest in the world. Other United States cities with subways are Chicago, Philadelphia, San Francisco, and Washington, DC.

San Francisco has a very new subway system. The trains travel in a tunnel under San Francisco Bay to the nearby cities of Oakland and Berkeley.

There is a big difference between a modern subway and an old one. The rubber wheels of the new subway trains make the trains very quiet. An old subway train can be very noisy and unpleasant. Still, a noisy subway train is faster than a car in traffic on the street above.

Downtown Montreal is a mix of old and new.

Open spaces were becoming smaller and smaller. The city grew more crowded.

The second time of growth began in the 1960s. A World's Fair was held in Montreal. More than 50 million people from all over the world came to Montreal for the fair. The fair was a great success.

Much building and rebuilding took place during this time. Better roads were built. A new subway was finished. The subway trains had rubber wheels. That way, they would not make much noise. Brightly colored pictures were painted on the walls underground. The Montreal subway is still one of the quietest in the world. It is one of the most beautiful, too.

New hotels, offices, and stores were built in downtown Montreal. Even Old Montreal was changed. This time, the old buildings were rebuilt to look the way they did long ago.

This time of growth continued into the 1970s. In 1976, the Olympic Games were held in Montreal. A large new sports stadium was built. Apartments were built for the athletes. After the Olympics, people rented the apartments.

REVIEW

CHECK YOUR FACTS

1. When did the first recent time of change begin in Montreal?
2. How did the city begin to change after 1945?
3. What important event took place in Montreal in the 1960s?
4. Montreal's subway is (noisy/quiet).
5. What event took place in Montreal in 1976?

THINK ABOUT IT

How can a fair or the Olympic Games help a city?

Lesson 3: What Do the People of Montreal Want?

Montreal continues to change. Many people are working to make Montreal a better place in which to live. Some people believe it is very important to save the old areas. These people are interested in the city's history. They care about the beautiful buildings built long ago. So they work with the government to save and rebuild them.

Other groups want to create new spaces. There are some very poor neighborhoods in Montreal. They are run-down. There are not enough low-cost houses or apartments. Some people want to build tall apartment buildings there. These buildings would have enough living space for a lot of people. Other people want to fix the old buildings that are falling apart. Both of these plans cost money.

Some groups try to help by telling people about their community. They write books about Montreal. Newspapers write stories about the needs of the city. People on television discuss the city's problems. All these things help the people of Montreal make better decisions for the future.

Left: This old house has been fixed up.
Below: Montreal has tall new buildings with many apartments in them.

REVIEW

CHECK YOUR FACTS

1. Some people are concerned about Montreal's history. What do they try to save?
2. There (are/are no) very poor neighborhoods in Montreal.
3. There (are/are not) enough low-cost houses and apartments in Montreal.
4. Why do some people want to build tall apartment buildings in Montreal?
5. Why is it important for people to learn more about their community?

THINK ABOUT IT

Which is better, fixing up old buildings or building new ones? Give reasons for your answer.

Lesson 4: The Future

NEW WORD

architect

You have learned about the basic needs people have. People's basic needs are staying alive, feeling safe, and feeling good about themselves.

The places where people live must help fill these needs. The air should be free of pollution. There should be enough food for everyone. Homes should protect people from the cold and heat. Streets and buildings should be made safe. Fire fighters and police should protect places from fires and crime. There should be spaces for being alone. There should be spaces to share with others. There should be places to see beautiful things. There should be places to relax and play.

Some people today are thinking very carefully about the future. They want to plan for people's needs. They want to plan for the needs of a big city 20, 50, and 100 years from now.

Some of these people work in the government. Some are architects (AHR kuh TEKTS). An **architect** draws up the plans for a new building or community. Others are simply citizens. But they all are people who care about what happens to their community.

Moshe Safdie (MOH shuh SAHF dee) is an architect. Some years ago, he decided to build special kinds of homes. Nothing like them had been built before. Moshe Safdie cared about two things very much. He cared about feeling and seeing the changes of the seasons. He liked to feel as though he were indoors and outdoors at the same time. The feeling of being in a big space was also important to him.

Here is what Moshe Safdie built. He called it Habitat. It is a building with 158 apartments.

Right: Moshe Safdie built Habitat.
Below: Cranes lift more apartments onto the top of Habitat.

How could he do this in a crowded city like Montreal?

First, each apartment was made separately. Plumbing and electricity were put in each. A giant crane then lifted each apartment. It rested the apartment on top of the one below.

Each apartment has an outdoor area. The windows are large. There are no indoor hallways. Instead, hallways between apartments are open to the air.

Look at the map on page 205. Can you find Habitat? It is on an island in the St. Lawrence River. The people who live in Habitat have a very special view of Montreal. They agree with Moshe Safdie. They have the feeling of being in a big space. Their apartments were made for living close to nature.

Left: A crane lifts an apartment.
Below: Habitat looks like a hill of pretty shapes.

REVIEW

CHECK YOUR FACTS

1. Name three basic kinds of needs people have.
2. What do architects do?
3. Who planned Habitat?
4. Where is Habitat?
5. The hallways between the apartments in Habitat are (open/closed).

THINK ABOUT IT

Would you like to live in a place like Habitat? Why, or why not?

CHAPTER REVIEW

CHECK YOUR FACTS

1. What province is Montreal in?
2. Name the river that flows past Montreal.
3. Montreal (is/is not) a port.
4. Name some things that make Montreal an important transportation center.
5. Name an important park in Montreal.
6. The World's Fair in Montreal (was/was not) a success.
7. What important means of transportation was built in Montreal in the 1960s?
8. When were the Olympic Games held in Montreal?
9. In Montreal, some people (are/are not) trying to save old buildings.
10. What did Moshe Safdie build?

USE YOUR MAP

11. Look at the map of the Montreal central business district on page 205. How many universities can you find?
12. How many bridges are shown on the map?
13. Does the Montreal subway go near Habitat?
14. In what square is the main post office located?
15. What important building is in square *C1*?

TRY SOMETHING NEW

16. Write a letter to a travel agency or airline. Try to get some tourist information on Montreal.
17. Write a short paper. Tell why you think old buildings should or should not be saved.

UNIT REVIEW

WATCH YOUR WORDS

1. Canada is divided into ___ and territories.
   provinces states environments
2. People must ___ to their environment.
   custom adapt measure up
3. In Dawson, vegetables are grown in ___.
   provinces plantations greenhouses
4. ___ are people who design plans for new buildings or communities.
   Innuit Architects Mayors

CHECK YOUR FACTS

5. What is the winter weather like in Canada?
6. How many provinces does Canada have?
7. Canada and the United States (do/do not) trade with each other.
8. Canada has (more/fewer) people than the United States.
9. What language do more than half of the Canadians speak?
10. Canada (does/does not) border on both the Atlantic Ocean and the Pacific Ocean.
11. What is the name of the capital city of Canada?
12. In what province do many French people live?
13. Farming (is/is not) important to Canada.
14. What is the name of the capital city of Ontario?
15. Most Canadians live in the (north/south).
16. Which way does the Trans-Canada Highway cross the country? From east to west or from north to south?
17. Are there more people in Dawson or in Victoria?
18. In what province is Montreal located?
19. What language do most people in Montreal speak?
20. What river connects Montreal to the Great Lakes and the Atlantic Ocean?
21. Montreal grew very fast just (before/after) 1945.
22. Name two important events that took place in Montreal in recent years.
23. Montreal's subway is (noisy/quiet).
24. Where is Habitat located?

CLOSE THE MAP GAP

25. Use an outline map of North America. Show and label the United States, Canada, and Mexico. Also include the Atlantic Ocean, the Pacific Ocean, and the Gulf of Mexico.
26. Use an outline map of Canada. Show and label each province.

USE YOUR MAPS

27. Look at the map of North America on page 185. What oceans does Alaska border on?
28. Look at the map of Canada on page 187. What province has land both on the continent and on an island?
29. Look at the population map of Canada on page 199. What two provinces seem to have the most people?
30. Look at the map of the Montreal central business district on page 205. What kinds of transportation can you find?
31. In what square is a museum located?

THINK ABOUT IT

32. In what ways is Canada like the United States? In what ways is it different?
33. Why does Canada have fewer people than the United States?
34. Some Innuit live in a part of the United States. Can you guess where?
35. You have studied the Eastern, Middle, and Western United States. How would you divide Canada into parts?
36. Some people in Quebec want to separate from Canada. They want to form a new nation. Why do you think they want to do this?

TRY SOMETHING NEW

37. Make a chart. List the provinces and territories of Canada and their capitals. You can find the names of the capitals in an encyclopedia.
38. Pick one of the Canadian provinces or territories. Use an encyclopedia to find out more about it. Then write a report about it.
39. The War of 1812 was the last time Canada and the United States fought. Write a report about it. Use an encyclopedia or other source suggested by your teacher.

PUT IT ALL TOGETHER

40. Make a chart that compares the United States and Canada. Use these headings: Populations, Parts, Capitals, Languages. Under "Population," put the number of people in each nation. Under "Parts," put the number of states in the United States. For Canada, put the number of provinces and the number of territories. Under "Capitals," name the capital cities of each nation. Under "Languages," list the main language or languages spoken in each. Use this book as your source of facts. Add other headings and facts suggested by your teacher.

OUR SOUTHERN NEIGHBOR

UNIT 5

CHAPTER 1 LOOKING AT MEXICO

Lesson 1: Mexico's Land

NEW WORDS
- plateau
- peninsula

Mexico is our southern neighbor. It is a nation, like the United States and Canada. Mexico has its own land, people, and government.

Mexico is smaller than the United States. It has only about one-fifth as much land. But it has about one-third as many people. Look at the bar graphs on page 221. They compare the United States, Canada, and Mexico. Notice that Mexico has more people than Canada. But Mexico has much less land.

All of Mexico lies south of the United States. Mexico and the United States have a very long

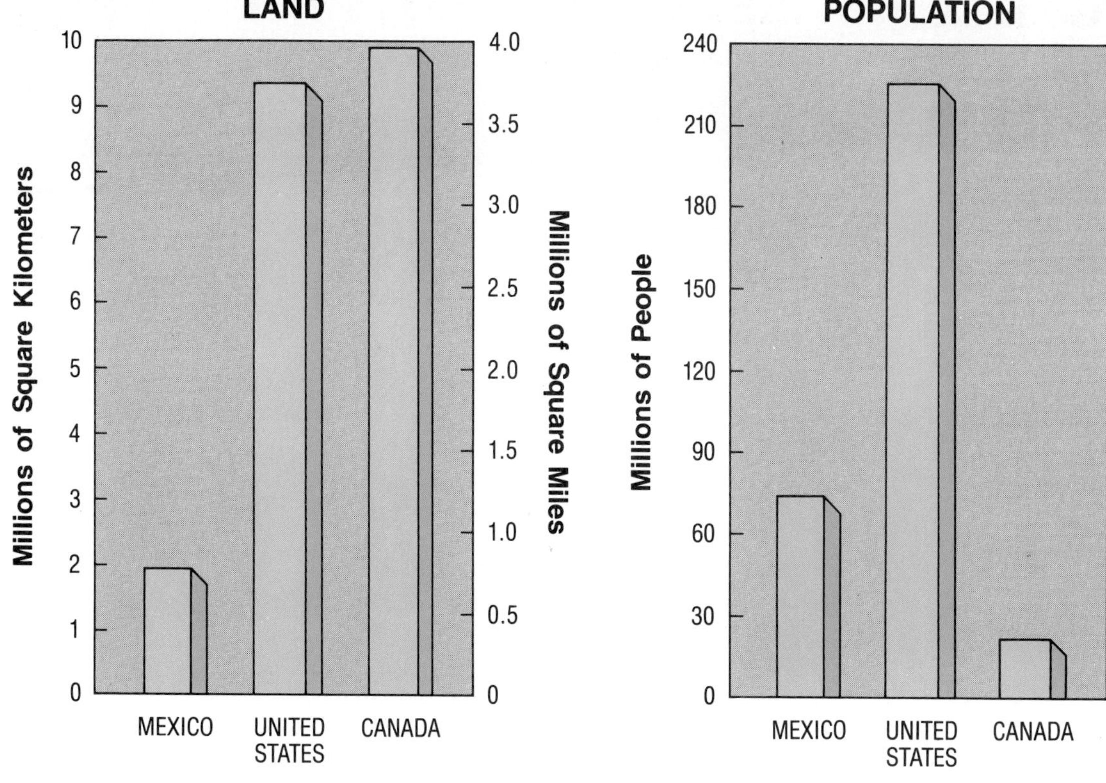

border. A river, the Rio Grande, forms a large part of this border. *Rio Grande* means "great river" in Spanish. Spanish is the main language spoken in Mexico.

Look at the map of Mexico on page 222. Notice that Mexico has coasts on the Pacific Ocean and the Gulf of Mexico. In that way, it is like the United States. But Mexico does not have many large cities along its coasts. In that way, it is different from the United States.

Most of Mexico's people live in the middle part of the nation. This area is called the central plateau (pla TOH). A **plateau** is an area of high, flat land. It is much like a plain, but it is higher.

WHERE WE ARE IN TIME AND PLACE

TIME LINE FOR MEXICO

1000 B.C.	300 A.D.	900 A.D.	1400s
Olmecs live in southeastern Mexico	Maya begin building great cities in the Yucatán	Maya begin leaving their cities	Aztecs build great empire in central Mexico

1519–1521	1810	1821	1917
Cortés conquers the Aztecs for Spain	Mexican Revolution begins	Mexico becomes independent from Spain	New constitution brings peace and order to Mexico

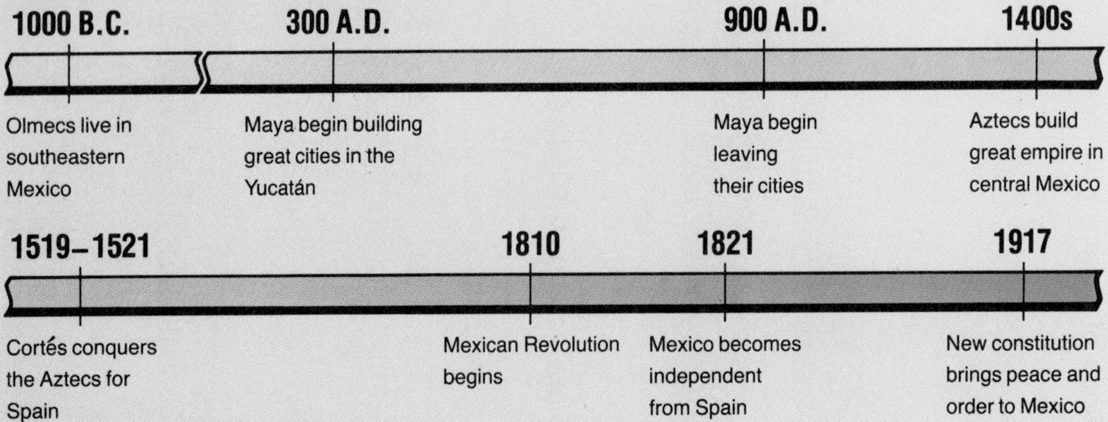

POLITICAL MAP OF MEXICO

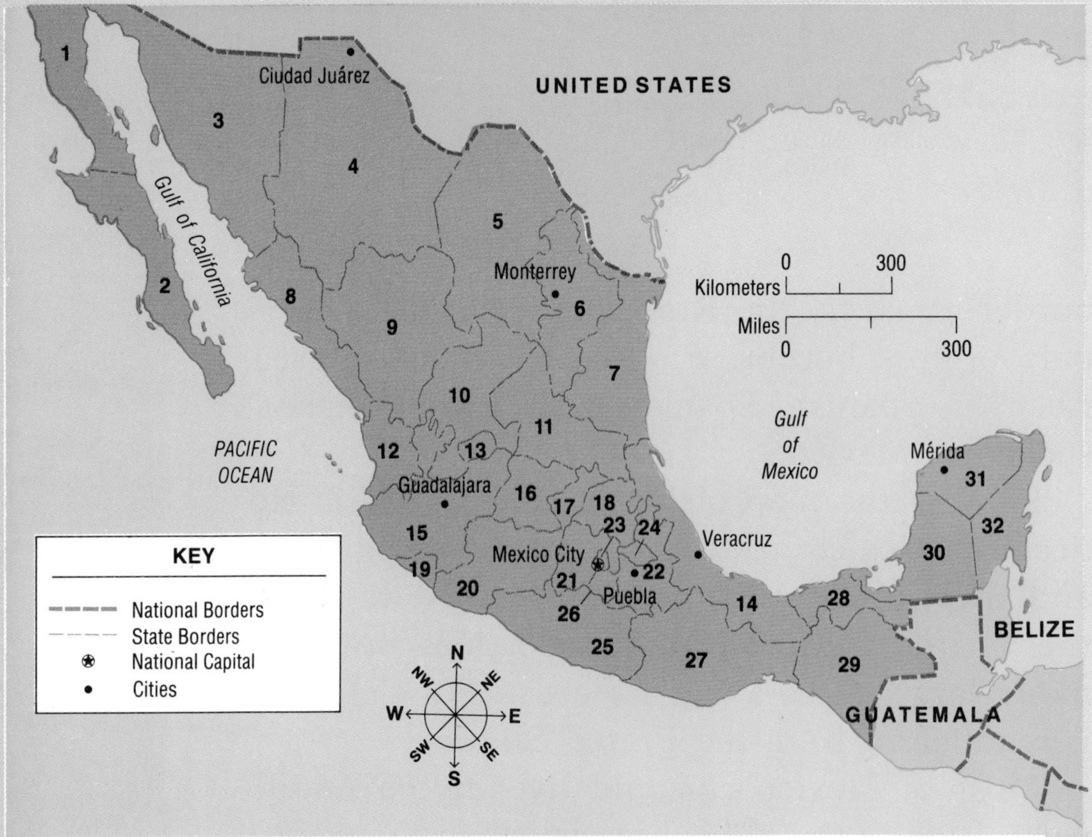

UNITED STATES
Ciudad Juárez
Gulf of California
Monterrey
PACIFIC OCEAN
Gulf of Mexico
Guadalajara
Mexico City
Puebla
Veracruz
Mérida
BELIZE
GUATEMALA
Kilometers
0
300
Miles
0
300
KEY
National Borders
State Borders
National Capital
Cities
N
NE
E
SE
S
SW
W
NW
1
2
3
4
5
6
7
8
9
10
11
12
13
14
15
16
17
18
19
20
21
22
23
24
25
26
27
28
29
30
31
32

STATES OF MEXICO

1. Baja California Norte
2. Baja California Sur
3. Sonora
4. Chihuahua
5. Coahuila
6. Nuevo León
7. Tamaulipas
8. Sinaloa
9. Durango
10. Zacatecas
11. San Luis Potosí
12. Nayarit
13. Aguascalientes
14. Veracruz
15. Jalisco
16. Guanajuato
17. Querétaro
18. Hidalgo
19. Colima
20. Michoacán
21. México
22. Puebla
23. Distrito Federal
24. Tlaxcala
25. Guerrero
26. Morelos
27. Oaxaca
28. Tabasco
29. Chiapas
30. Campeche
31. Yucatán
32. Quintana Roo

A big part of Mexico is covered by the central plateau. This plateau has some good soil for farming. The weather is not too hot or too cold. There is also enough rain for crops to grow.

High mountains separate the central plateau from the coasts. Along the coasts are areas of low land. All of these lowlands are hot. Most are dry. But one area has much rain and thick forests. This area is on the southeast coast. It is called the Yucatán Peninsula (YOO kuh TAN puh NIN suh luh). A **peninsula** is a piece of land almost surrounded by water.

Like our nation, Mexico is divided into states. Mexico has 31 states. It also has a federal district. The capital of Mexico is in the federal district. Mexico City is the capital of Mexico. The government of the nation meets there.

REVIEW

WATCH YOUR WORDS

1. An area of high, flat land is a___.
   peninsula border plateau
2. A piece of land almost surrounded by water is a___.
   plateau peninsula state

CHECK YOUR FACTS

Look at the Bar Graphs

3. About how big is Mexico?
4. About how many people does Mexico have?

Look at the Lesson

5. What river forms much of the border between the United States and Mexico?
6. Where do most of Mexico's people live?
7. How many states are there in Mexico?

THINK ABOUT IT

Why do few people live along Mexico's coasts?

Lesson 2: The People of Mexico

NEW WORD

village

Long ago, American Indians were the only people who lived in Mexico. Then, people started to come to Mexico from Europe. About 450 years ago, people came to Mexico from Spain. Spain was the first European nation to send settlers to the Americas. Later, some people came to Mexico from Africa and Asia.

Today, most Mexicans are mestizos. You read about mestizos when you studied the history of Los Angeles. Mestizos are people who are part Spanish and part American Indian. About 67 of every 100 Mexicans are mestizos. About 25 of every 100 are American Indians. Most of the other Mexicans are Spanish. Look at the pie graph on page 225. It shows the size of the different groups in Mexico.

About 10 out of 15 people in Mexico live in cities. In the United States, about 12 out of every 15 live in cities.

The rest of Mexico's people live outside the cities. Most live in small villages. A **village** is a community smaller than a town. The village people in Mexico are mostly farmers. They live near their fields. Today, many people in Mexico are leaving the villages. They are going to the cities to look for work.

In Mexico, the population is growing very fast. Each year, the population gets bigger. So each year, Mexico needs to produce more goods and services. Otherwise, there will be less for

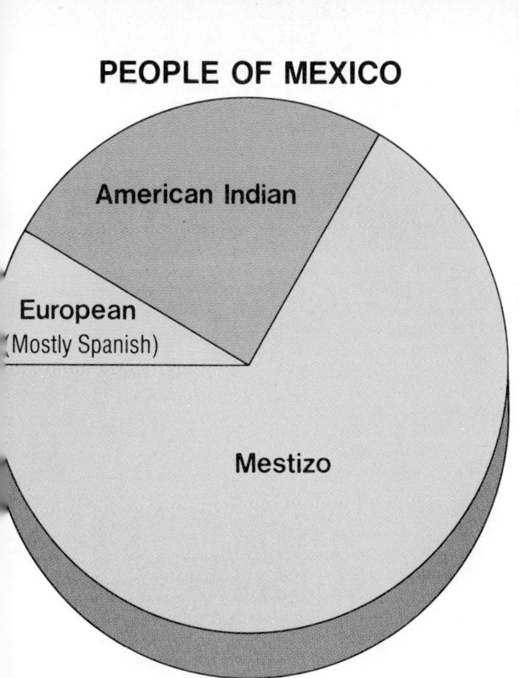

People wait for the bus in a Mexican town.

each person. Another thing must happen as the number of people grows. The number of jobs must grow, too. Unless there are more jobs, many people will not have work. They will have no way to earn a living.

REVIEW

CHECK YOUR FACTS

1. What people lived in Mexico first?
2. What people came to Mexico about 450 years ago?
3. Do most Mexicans live in cities or in villages?
4. Are Mexicans leaving their villages or going back to them?
5. Is Mexico's population getting larger or smaller?

THINK ABOUT IT

Suppose the population of Mexico keeps growing. Suppose the number of goods, services, and jobs does not grow. What will happen?

Lesson 3: Mexico's Resources

NEW WORD

mineral

These nurses are on their way to the hospital where they work.

Each year, Mexico must provide more goods and services. Mexican businesses must create more jobs. That means that Mexicans have to build more factories and offices. They have to build more schools and hospitals. They have to build more homes and roads. People need resources to build and run all these things. They need large amounts of money as well.

Mexico is rich in natural resources. It has many minerals. It has some good farmland. It has some forests. It usually has good weather all year long.

There are many different kinds of land in Mexico. Much of the land is dry. There are many mountains. But there is also much good farmland in the central plateau. Mexican farmers grow many vegetables and fruits. They grow large crops of corn, squash, and beans. They grow wheat and sugar cane. They grow cotton and coffee, too. In some dry places, farmers bring water to the land. With water, they can grow crops there. In other dry places, farmers raise cattle and sheep.

Mexico has many useful minerals. A **mineral** is something in nature that is not an animal or plant. Minerals are taken from the ground. Mexico has minerals such as gold and silver. It has minerals such as copper, lead, iron ore, and coal. What is more, Mexico has a lot of petroleum. It sells much petroleum to other nations. The money from petroleum helps Mexico grow.

The weather is also an important resource for Mexico. It is warm all year. Mexico has beautiful coasts and beaches. The nation also has a very rich history. Because of these things, many tourists go to Mexico. They spend a lot of money

The Yucatán Peninsula has beautiful beaches.

This outdoor market has all kinds of fruits and vegetables.

there. This money helps Mexico. Tourists also help create new jobs. Mexican workers provide services for tourists and sell them goods.

Today, many Mexicans are poor. Many people do not have enough work to earn a living. Mexico has not become as rich as the United States and Canada. But Mexico is growing fast. And it is making a lot of progress.

REVIEW

CHECK YOUR FACTS

1. What two things are needed for building factories?
2. Where in Mexico is there much good farmland?
3. What mineral does Mexico sell in large amounts to other nations?
4. How is the weather a good resource for Mexico?
5. How do tourists help create jobs?

TRY SOMETHING NEW

6. Put each group of resources into the right class.

(1). corn, squash, and cotton	**A.** animal
(2). petroleum, iron ore, and coal	**B.** vegetable
(3). sheep and cattle	**C.** mineral

7. Get some tourist information about Mexico. Look in magazines, or write a travel agency or airline.

CHAPTER REVIEW

WATCH YOUR WORDS

Fill in the blanks. Choose a word from the list below.

1. A ___ is a piece of land almost surrounded by water.
2. A ___ is an area of high, flat land.
3. A ___ is a community smaller than a town.
4. A ___ is taken from the ground.

mineral peninsula plateau village

CHECK YOUR FACTS

5. Which nation has more people, Canada or Mexico?
6. What is the capital of Mexico?
7. What nation of Europe sent many settlers to Mexico?
8. Most Mexicans are (mestizos/Spanish).
9. List two crops and two animals raised in Mexico.
10. List four mineral resources of Mexico.

USE YOUR GRAPHS AND MAP

11. Look at the bar graphs on page 221. Rank Mexico, the United States, and Canada by size. Then rank them by number of people.
12. Look at the map of Mexico on page 222. What countries border on Mexico?
13. Are the larger Mexican states in the north or in the south?
14. Name the state in which Mérida is located.
15. Look at the pie graph of the Mexican people on page 225. List the groups in order of size.

THINK ABOUT IT

16. Much of the United States once belonged to Mexico. Was the place where you live ever part of Mexico?
17. The United States is five times larger than Mexico. It has three times as many people as Mexico. Which nation is more crowded?
18. The higher an area is, the cooler its weather tends to be. How does this fact explain where most Mexicans live?
19. What peninsulas in the United States can you name?
20. Most people in the United States and Canada are of European background. How do the people of Mexico differ?

TRY SOMETHING NEW

21. Tourists need many services. They also like to buy goods. Make a list of goods and services that tourists buy.

CHAPTER 2 HISTORY OF MEXICO

Lesson 1: American Indians of Long Ago

NEW WORDS

pyramid
temple
priest
scholar
tortilla

The history of Mexico is very long. It begins thousands of years ago with American Indians.

One of the most important early groups was the Maya (MAH yuh). They lived in the Yucatán Peninsula. They also lived in lands south of Mexico. About 1700 years ago, the Maya began building great cities of stone. In these cities, they built tall pyramids. A **pyramid** is a building with sides that slant up to the top. The Mayan pyramids had flat tops. On top, the Maya built small temples. A **temple** is a religious building. **Priests,** or religious leaders, climbed long staircases to the temples. There, they prayed to their gods.

Mayan priests were also scholars (SKOL urs). **Scholars** are people who study and learn. The priests studied the stars, the moon, and the sun. They knew how the sun, stars, and moon moved in the sky. They knew the year was 365 days long. They made a calendar as good as the one we have today.

Mayan scholars also studied math. The Maya knew as much about math as any other people of their time. They also had a special kind of writing. The words were made up of little pictures. The Maya made paper to write on from tree bark. They also carved records of important events on large stone monuments.

STRANGE FACTS

The Maya built great cities. They lived and worked in those cities for about 600 years. Then they began to leave the cities. Experts have spent years trying to figure out why. Did a terrible disease make the cities unsafe? Did the crops fail? Did the climate change? Did farmers stop growing enough food to feed the city people? No one knows for sure.

A Mexican woman is making tortillas.

The Maya were a peaceful people. Mayan farmers grew corn, beans, and squash. They grew tomatoes and avocados. Corn was their most important food. The Maya made a flat corn cake. Now we call it a **tortilla** (tor TEE yuh).

The Mayan cities lasted for hundreds of years. Then, about 1000 years ago, the Maya began leaving their cities. No one knows why this happened. The forests grew over the pyramids and other stone buildings. Today, only the ruins of the Mayan cities remain. But some people in Mexico still speak Mayan languages.

REVIEW

WATCH YOUR WORDS

1. A___is a corn cake.
   scholar tortilla pyramid
2. A___has sides that slant up to the top.
   temple tortilla pyramid
3. A___is a religious leader.
   temple priest pyramid
4. A___is a religious building.
   temple priest scholar
5. A___studies and learns.
   pyramid temple scholar

CHECK YOUR FACTS

6. Where in Mexico did the Maya live?
7. What did the Maya build?
8. What did the Mayan scholars study?
9. What kind of writing did the Maya have?
10. What happened to the Mayan cities?

THINK ABOUT IT

How did farming make the Mayan cities possible?

Lesson 2: The Aztec Empire

NEW WORDS

empire

causeway

Another American Indian people in Mexico were the Aztecs. During the 1400s, the Aztecs began building an empire. An **empire** is a group of lands under one government. The Aztec capital was named Tenochtitlán (teh NOCH teet LAHN). It stood where Mexico City stands today. At first, the Aztecs ruled only the land around their city. Then, they began adding to their empire. Soon it stretched west to the Pacific Ocean. It stretched east to the Gulf of Mexico.

The Aztec capital, Tenochtitlán, was built on an island. This island was in the middle of a large lake. Four **causeways**, or raised roads, connected the island to the mainland. People and goods were also moved in canoes.

The Aztecs sold many fine things in their markets.

In 1519, 11 ships arrived off the coast of Mexico. They were large wooden ships with tall sails. The American Indians had never seen such ships before.

Off the ships came even stranger sights. White men came ashore riding large animals. The men wore shiny armor. They carried noisy weapons that could kill people at a distance. The Indians had never seen horses and guns before.

Some Indians sent messages about these strange sights to the Aztec ruler. The ruler's name was Montezuma (MON tuh ZOO muh). He did not know what to do about these strangers. He feared their leader might be a god. There was an old Aztec story about a god who sailed away. The god was supposed to return from the sea. Montezuma sent gifts of gold and silver to the strangers. He also told them to leave Mexico.

The strangers were Spanish. Their leader was Hernando Cortés (kor TEZ). He had an army of

500 men and 16 horses. He was looking for treasure, land, and power. Cortés saw Montezuma's rich gifts. He decided to go to the Aztec capital. Along the way, Indians who were enemies of the Aztecs joined Cortés. They hoped he would destroy the Aztecs.

This shield made from feathers belonged to Montezuma.

Cortés arrived at Tenochtitlán in November of 1519. Montezuma welcomed Cortés with many gifts. But Cortés wanted more than gifts. He wanted to rule the Aztec empire. He took Montezuma captive. His soldiers began taking gold from the Aztecs. The Spanish also wanted the Aztecs to become Christians. So they began destroying the Aztec temples.

Soon the Aztecs rose up. They drove the Spanish from the city. They destroyed most of the Spanish army. For a while, it seemed that Cortés had been defeated. But he had many American Indian followers. More soldiers also arrived from Spain. In 1521, Cortés and his army attacked Tenochtitlán. Thousands of Aztecs were killed. Soon the city fell. Cortés and his army destroyed it.

In the next few months, Cortés conquered the whole Aztec empire. He ruled in the name of the king of Spain. For the next 300 years, Mexico belonged to Spain, a nation in Europe.

Cortés sees the Aztec capital in the distance.

REVIEW

CHECK YOUR FACTS

1. In what year did Cortés arrive in Mexico?
2. Who was the ruler of the Aztecs when Cortés arrived?
3. Why did the Spanish destroy the Aztec temples?
4. What nation ruled Mexico after Cortés conquered it?

THINK ABOUT IT

How could Cortés and his small army conquer the powerful and rich Aztec empire?

Lesson 3: Spanish Rule in Mexico

NEW WORDS

- colony
- estate
- slave
- viceroy
- creole

The Spanish called their colony of Mexico *New Spain*. A **colony** is an area of land ruled by another nation. Mexico was actually much larger than Spain itself. But the Spanish king simply used Mexico to make Spain richer. For many years, huge amounts of treasure were sent from Mexico to Spain.

The king gave the conquerers of Mexico great estates. An **estate** is a very large piece of land. He also gave estates to his friends. The king included in the estates the American Indians who lived on the land. The king's friends also were in charge of the mines.

The American Indians in Mexico were forced to work on estates and in mines. Sometimes, there were not enough of them to do the work. In that case, Black people from Africa were brought in as slaves. A **slave** is a person who is owned by another person. The American Indians and Blacks had no rights under Spanish rule.

The government of New Spain was headed by a leader called a **viceroy.** The viceroy came from Spain. He was chosen by the king. He ruled in the king's name. Only people born in Spain could have important jobs in the government of the colony. Over the years, new leaders were sent from Spain to Mexico.

Spanish people born in Mexico could hold only the less important government jobs. The Spanish people born in Mexico had a special name. They were called **creoles** (KREE OHLZ). Creoles resented the people born in Spain. Mestizos had fewer rights than creoles. They could be only farmers, skilled workers, or laborers. They could not hold government jobs.

Many people in New Spain began to resent the rule of Spain. Creoles did not like being ruled by people born in Europe. Mestizos, American Indians, and Blacks had no way to improve their lives. But for almost 300 years, Spain was strong enough to hold on to Mexico.

The Spanish built this great church in Mexico City.

REVIEW

WATCH YOUR WORDS

1. A(n)___ is a very large piece of land.
   creole viceroy estate
2. A ___ is a person owned by another.
   creole tortilla slave
3. The ruler of New Spain was the___.
   estate viceroy creole
4. A ___ is an area of land ruled by another nation.
   plateau viceroy colony
5. A(n)___ was a Spanish person born in New Spain.
   creole viceroy estate

CHECK YOUR FACTS

6. What did the Spanish call Mexico?
7. Where did the Spanish make the American Indians work?
8. Who headed the government of New Spain?
9. Why did the creoles, mestizos, American Indians, and Blacks resent Spanish rule?

TRY SOMETHING NEW

Make a chart of the groups of people in New Spain. Include Spanish born in Spain, creoles, mestizos, American Indians, and Blacks. Show what kinds of jobs each group could hold.

Lesson 4: Mexico Becomes Independent

Mexicans celebrate September 16 as their independence day. They begin the celebration the night before. Late at night on September 15, 1810, a Mexican priest gave a famous speech. His name was Miguel Hidalgo (mee GEHL ee THAHL goh). In his speech, he called for freedom from Spain. Hidalgo and his followers began a war for independence. But they were not a real army. They were not trained as soldiers. In 1811,

Miguel Hidalgo wanted Mexico to be free.

Hidalgo was captured by Spanish soldiers and killed.

After a long struggle, Mexico became independent from Spain in 1821. For almost 100 years, different groups struggled for power in Mexico. Government leaders were often changed by fighting rather than by voting.

Then, in 1917, Mexico approved a new constitution. This was the beginning of great changes in Mexico. The government became stronger. It had better control of the nation.

In the following years, the government broke up the big estates. It gave much land to the poor American Indians and mestizos. It started schools in the villages. It improved roads and health care. The new government was willing to spend money to improve Mexico.

REVIEW

CHECK YOUR FACTS

1. What is the Mexican independence day?
2. Who made a speech in 1810 calling for freedom from Spain?
3. In what year did Mexico become independent?
4. List three things the Mexican government did in the years after 1917.

THINK ABOUT IT

What nation declared its independence on July 4, 1776? Was Mexico independent then?

CHAPTER REVIEW

WATCH YOUR WORDS

1. The Maya built great___.
   empires pyramids causeways
2. A(n)___is a religious building.
   temple pyramid empire
3. A___is a religious leader.
   viceroy priest scholar
4. The Aztecs ruled a large___.
   colony estate empire
5. A(n)___is a raised road.
   plateau estate causeway
6. The king of Spain gave his friends great___in Mexico.
   pyramids estates colonies
7. The Spanish brought Blacks from Africa to Mexico as___.
   slaves viceroys creoles
8. The ___ were Spanish people born in Mexico.
   viceroys creoles slaves
9. New Spain was ruled by a___.
   priest creole viceroy
10. New Spain was a(n) ___ of Spain.
    estate colony empire

CHECK YOUR FACTS

11. List five things the Maya did.
12. What people built their capital city on an island?
13. Who led the Spanish conquest of Mexico?
14. What did the Spanish call Mexico?
15. What did Miguel Hidalgo do? What happened to him?

THINK ABOUT IT

16. Why do nations celebrate their independence day?

CHAPTER 3 MEXICO CITY

Lesson 1: The Heart of Mexico

Mexico City is the capital of Mexico. It is the largest city in the Americas. It is the second-largest city in the world. Only Shanghai (shang HY) in China is larger. Over 9 million people live in Mexico City. About 12 million people live in the urban area.

Mexico City is very much the heart of Mexico. The government of the nation meets there. The city is the center of education for Mexico. It is

STRANGE FACTS

Chapultepec (chuh POOL tuh PEHK) Park is in Mexico City. It was first used by the Aztecs. Today, the park has flower gardens, fountains, a zoo, and many trees. The park also has a high hill called Chapultepec Hill. At the bottom of the hill is a building that tells a sad story.

In 1847, the United States and Mexico were at war. American soldiers were fighting their way into Mexico City. Mexican soldiers on Chapultepec Hill blocked their way.

These Mexican soldiers were boys who were still students at a school for soldiers. They fought bravely, but the Americans were too strong. The boys did not want to surrender. Instead, they took hold of the Mexican flag. Then, holding the flag, the boys jumped off the hill to their deaths.

Now, at the foot of the hill, there is the Monument to the Boy Heroes. It honors the young Mexican soldiers who gave up their lives for their country.

the center of the tourist trade. It is also the center of transportation and of industry.

The center of Mexico City itself is called Constitution Plaza. It is built where the main plaza of the Aztecs once was. Around it are many famous buildings. Among them are the National Palace, the National Cathedral, and the Supreme Court. The offices of Mexico's president are in the National Palace.

Mexico City is built where Tenochtitlán once stood. Remember, the Aztec capital was on an island in a lake. As Mexico City grew, the lake was drained and filled in. Today, the lake is gone. But many parts of the city are on soil that has a lot of water in it. Some parts of the city have been sinking slowly for many years.

Mexico City is located in the Valley of Mexico. This is a big valley shaped like a bowl. It is surrounded by mountains. There are no rivers to carry rainwater out of the valley. So the government had to build canals. Canals carry away rainwater. Without the canals, Mexico City would have great floods.

Mexico City is a mixture of old and new. Ruins of old American Indian temples are near the city. These temples were built long before the Aztecs ruled. In the city are many beautiful palaces and churches built by the Spanish. Nearby are many tall modern buildings. The modern buildings are often built with flat walls. The walls are then covered with beautiful paintings. This kind of painting was done long ago by the Maya and the Aztecs. The Plaza of Three Cultures says much about Mexico. It has Aztec ruins, Spanish buildings, and modern apartment houses.

REVIEW

CHECK YOUR FACTS

1. About how many people live in Mexico City?
2. What is the center of Mexico City?
3. What happened to the lake around Tenochtitlán?
4. In what valley is Mexico City located?
5. Mexico City (does/does not) have modern buildings.

THINK ABOUT IT

Suppose you could visit Mexico City. What place or places would you most like to see?

Lesson 2: Mexico City and the Future

Almost half of all the goods manufactured in Mexico are made in Mexico City. The city has thousands of factories. Many different kinds of goods are made in these factories. Automobiles, clothing, and iron and steel products are made here. More factories are being built each year. Businesses are growing. But all this activity is causing problems in Mexico City.

Each year, thousands of people come to Mexico City to live. They come to look for jobs. But many do not have skills. So they can get only low-paying jobs. Or they can get no jobs at all. These people and their families are very poor. If they are to get jobs, they must be trained. Their children need schools. They need houses and health care. All these things cost money.

Mexico City has many new factories.

Some people in Mexico City are very poor.

Mexico City has a new subway.

Once, Mexico City was known for its pure air. Today, a great blanket of dirty air hangs over the city. Cars, trucks, and factories pour wastes into the air. The polluted air is trapped in the bowl-shaped valley. Winds do not blow it away.

Traffic is a big problem in Mexico City. This is true in many large cities. In the past few years, the government of Mexico City has built a subway. It is clean and modern. Millions of people ride it every day. This subway helps cut down on traffic jams.

Each year, thousands of students come to Mexico City. Many come to attend the National University. It was founded in 1551. That makes it the oldest university in the Americas. Today, more than 100,000 students go to school there.

The past and the present meet in Mexico City. The future may bring answers to the city's problems. Mexico City is still growing fast. Soon, it may be the largest city in the world!

REVIEW

CHECK YOUR FACTS

1. Mexico City (does/does not) have many factories.
2. Why do many people who come to Mexico City have trouble finding jobs?
3. What two problems do cars and trucks cause?
4. What has helped cut down on traffic problems in Mexico City?
5. Why do many students come to Mexico City?

THINK ABOUT IT

Does your community have any of the same problems Mexico City has? If so, which ones?

CHAPTER REVIEW

CHECK YOUR FACTS

1. What is the capital of Mexico?
2. What is the largest city in the Americas?
3. Who has offices in the National Palace in Mexico City?
4. Why are canals needed to carry rainwater out of the Valley of Mexico?
5. What three kinds of buildings can be seen in the Plaza of Three Cultures?
6. Name some goods that are made in Mexico City.
7. List three things the poor people of Mexico City need.
8. How did Mexico City's air get polluted?
9. What new form of transportation has been built in Mexico City?

THINK ABOUT IT

10. Some cities have problems when many people move there. Other cities have problems when many people leave. Which problems are worse?
11. Suppose you were digging the foundation for a building in Mexico City. What might you find?
12. In Mexico, the capital of the nation is also the largest city. Is this true in the United States and Canada?
13. In what ways is Mexico City the heart of Mexico?
14. Mexico City has many old and new buildings. There are other cities that are mostly new or mostly old. Which kind of city do you think is more interesting? Why?

UNIT REVIEW

WATCH YOUR WORDS

Use the words below to fill in the blanks. Use each term only once.

causeways	minerals	scholars
colony	Peninsula	slaves
creoles	plateau	temples
empire	priests	viceroy
estates	pyramids	villages

Most of Mexico's people live on the central ___. Few people live on the Yucatán ___. Outside the cities, most Mexicans live in small ___. Mexico is rich in natural resources such as ___. But many Mexicans remain poor.

Long ago, the Maya built tall ___ in southern Mexico. On the top of these were ___. There, Mayan ___ prayed to their gods. The Mayan priests were also ___.

The Aztecs created a great ___. Their capital was built on an island in a lake. It was connected to the mainland by ___.

The Spanish conquered Mexico and made it a(n) ___. They divided the land into large ___. American Indians and Black ___ worked on the land and in the mines. The government was headed by the ___ from Spain. The Spanish people born in Mexico were called ___.

CHECK YOUR FACTS

1. Which nation is larger, Mexico or Canada? Which has more people?
2. What bodies of water border Mexico?
3. What was the first European nation to send settlers to the Americas?
4. What is the largest group of people in Mexico? What is their background?
5. Why must Mexico create more jobs, goods, and services each year?
6. How is the climate an important resource for Mexico?
7. Where in Mexico did the Maya live?
8. What was the most important food of the Maya?
9. When did the Aztecs begin building their empire?
10. What city now stands where Tenochtitlán once stood?
11. Who was the Aztec ruler when the Spanish arrived?
12. Who helped Cortés against the Aztecs?

13. Who held the most important jobs in New Spain?
14. What religion did the Spanish bring to Mexico?
15. Why is September 16 an important day in Mexico?
16. What did Miguel Hidalgo and his followers do?
17. What is the capital of Mexico?
18. Is there still a lake around Mexico City?
19. What different kinds of buildings are in or near Mexico City?
20. The population of Mexico City (is/is not) growing.

THINK ABOUT IT

21. Which nation do you think has the best weather: the United States, Canada, or Mexico?
22. Why do most Mexicans live on the central plateau? Give as many reasons as you can.
23. Tenochtitlán was in the middle of a lake. A city in Italy is also surrounded by water. Do you know its name? What is it?
24. Why do you think the Aztecs were afraid of horses?
25. Where else were there slaves on the North American continent besides Mexico?
26. Mexico City is surrounded by mountains. How might this limit its growth some day?

CLOSE THE MAP GAP

27. You have studied two American Indian groups that lived in Mexico. They are the Maya and the Aztecs. Draw a map of Mexico that shows where the two groups lived.
28. Draw a map showing Mexico in 1821. Use an encyclopedia to see what the borders were then. Label the areas that are now a part of the United States.
29. Draw a map of North America. Show the three large nations and their capitals. Also show important bodies of water.

TRY SOMETHING NEW

30. Draw and color a picture of the Mexican flag.
31. July 4 is Independence Day in the United States. September 16 is the day the Mexicans celebrate their independence from Spain. Find out when a similar day is celebrated in Canada.
32. Write a report on one of the American Indian peoples who lived in Mexico long ago.

PUT IT ALL TOGETHER

33. Make a chart that compares the United States, Canada, and Mexico.

GLOSSARY

adapt to change when you need to (200)
aerial (AR ee ul) **photograph** a picture of Earth taken from the air (36)
aqueduct (AK wuh dukt) a waterway of pipes, tunnels, and canals. It carries water from one place to another. (151)
architect (AHR kuh TEKT) a person who draws up plans for buildings (213)
area **1** a place **2** the amount of land a place covers (25)

bar graph a picture that uses bars of different lengths to show amounts (29)
Bill of Rights a part of the Constitution of the United States. It says what the rights of the people are. (72)
border a line that divides one country or state from another (43)
boundary another word for BORDER (79)

capital a city where the government of a state or nation meets (43)
Capitol the building in Washington, DC, where Congress meets (64)
cardinal (KAHR duh nul) **directions** the four most important directions on Earth: north, south, east, and west (21)
causeway a raised road, as one built over water (233)
central business district the part of a city where almost all the land is used for offices and stores (97)
chart a picture or list that shows facts in a certain order (28)
choice one of two or more things a person can decide to do (112)
citizen a member of a nation, state, or city (170)
city a large town where a lot of people live and work (25)
city council a group of people elected to make laws for a city (161)
city manager a person hired by a city council to run the city government (161)
colony an area of land ruled by another nation (237)
commercial (kuh MUR shul) **land** land used for stores and office buildings (94)
community (kuh MYOO nuh tee) **1** a group of people living together in one place **2** the place where they live (23)
compass **1** on a map, a drawing with arrows that point in different directions (81) **2** a tool with a pointer that always points toward the North Pole (82)
Congress the part of the government that makes the laws for the United States (66)
Constitution (KON stuh TOO shun) the written agreement that set up the government of the United States (70)
consumer (kun SOO mur) a person who uses goods and services (104)
continent (KON tuh nunt) one of the seven large areas of land on Earth (15)
cost all the things a person gives up when making a choice (111)
country a group of people with their own government and land; a nation (42)
custom a way of doing things (176)

decision a final choice (113)
decision model a drawing that shows how different choices lead to different results (112)
desert a very dry place where few plants will grow (135)
direction which way something is. North, south, east, west, left, right, up, and down are directions. (18)
distance how far one place is from another (83)
distance scale a diagram that shows what a map distance equals in real distance (83)

district a part of a larger area, such as part of a city (161)

elect to choose (a leader) by voting (70)
empire a group of lands under one government (233)
energy power to do work or to run machines (117)
engine a machine that uses energy to do work (117)
estate a very large piece of land (237)
executive (eg ZEK yuh tiv) **branch** the branch of government that carries out the laws (71)

factory a building in which goods are made, especially with machines (56)
fuel something that produces heat energy when it is burned (117)

globe a round model of Earth (15)
goods things, such as food and clothes, that can be used or sold (102)
government **1** a system of laws and rules **2** a group of people that makes laws and rules (42)
grid lines on a map that crisscross and divide the map into squares (40)

harvest the bringing in of crops (50)
history the story of the past (47)
House of Representatives (REP ri ZEN tuh tivz) one of two parts of Congress (66)

industrial land land with factories and other places where things are made (94)
island a piece of land surrounded by water (135)

judicial (joo DISH ul) **branch** the branch of government that decides whether laws have been obeyed or broken (71)

lake a large body of water surrounded by land (79)
land-use map a map that shows how the land in an area is used (94)
legislative (LEJ iss LAY tiv) **branch** the branch of government that makes the laws (70)

map a flat drawing of Earth or part of Earth (38)
mayor the leader of a city (160)
means of transportation (TRANS pur TAY shun) the ways that people and goods move from place to place (116)
mineral something in nature that is not an animal or plant (227)
monument something, such as a building, that helps people remember a person or event (65)
mountain an area of land that is much higher than the land around it (43)
mountain range a group or row of mountains (43)

nation another word for COUNTRY (42)
natural environment the shape and location of the land, the weather, and the plants and animals of a place (137)
natural gas a mixture of gases found in the ground and used as a fuel (122)
natural resource something found on Earth that people can use (58)
North Pole the place that is farthest north on Earth (18)

occupation (OK yuh PAY shun) a job that a person does for a living (26)
ocean one of the four very large bodies of water on Earth (17)
oil another word for PETROLEUM (118)
oil field an area where petroleum is found (122)

peninsula (pen NIN syoo luh) a piece of land almost surrounded by water (223)

petrochemical (PET roh KEM i kul) a chemical made from petroleum and natural gas (124)
petroleum (puh TROH lee um) a thick, dark liquid found in the ground and used as a fuel; oil (117)
plain a big, open area of flat land (78)
plantation (plan TAY shun) a big farm where crops are grown (170)
plateau (pla TOH) a big area of high, flat land (221)
population (POP yuh LAY shun) the number of people who live in a place (25)
port a place where ships load and unload goods (125)
President the leader of the United States (66)
province a part of Canada that is like a state in the United States (186)
public land land that is owned by all the people. Places like schools and parks may be found on this land. (94)

refinery a factory where petroleum is made into useful products such as gasoline (123)
representative (REP ri ZEN tuh tiv) **1** a person chosen to act for a group **2** a member of the House of Representatives (71)
residential (REZ uh DEN chul) **land** land on which people live (94)
result what happens when a choice is made (112)
river a large, natural stream of water. It usually starts in the mountains and flows toward the sea. (79)

seacoast the land closest to the ocean (139)
Senate one of two parts of Congress (66)
senator a member of the Senate (71)
service an action that one person can do to fill the needs of another (103)
South Pole the place that is farthest south on Earth (18)
state one of 50 parts that make up the United States. Each state has its own land, people, and government (43)
stockyards large yards with pens where cattle, sheep, or pigs are kept before they are sent to market (92)
suburb a small community near a city (27)
Supreme Court the most powerful court in the United States (68)
symbol a picture on a map that stands for a real thing (38)

taxes money that people pay to support their government (106)
territory (TEHR uh TOR ee) part of a country that has less power than a state (170)
textiles woven cloth (56)
time line a line that shows the dates of important events (48)
town a community smaller than a city but larger than a village
transportation (TRANS pur TAY shun) **land** land used for roads, railroads, train or bus stations, and airports (96)

urban area a city and its suburbs (27)

vacant land land that is not being used yet (96)
valley a low area of land between mountains or hills (139)
village a community smaller than a town (224)

wagon train a group of wagons traveling together across the country (90)

zoning laws rules that say how land in cities may be used (127)

INDEX

CREDITS

8–13, 27, 44, 63, 141, 157, 171, 222: Maps by Continental Cartography. **28, 49, 63, 89, 141, 145, 171, 177, 187, 188, 221, 222, 225:** Charts and Time Lines by Function Thru Form Inc. **14:** NASA. **23:** Owen Franken/Stock, Boston. **24:** (BR) Bruno Barbey/Magnum; (Others) Adam Woofitt/Woodfin Camp. **26:** (TL) Raimondo Borea/Photo Researchers; (TR) Alec Duncan/Taurus. **30:** (BL) Alex Webb/Magnum; (BR) Kryn Traconis/Magnum. **31:** Owen Franken/Stock, Boston. **32:** (BL) Karen Cooledge/McGraw-Hill; (BR) Nick Passman/Stock, Boston. **43:** Nathan Benin/Woodfin Camp. **50:** NYPL Picture Collection. **52:** NYPL Picture Collection. **55:** Allen B. Commack. **56:** John King/McGraw-Hill. **57:** Brown Brothers. **58:** (BL) Grant Heilman; (BR) Joel A. Brown/FPG. **59:** Burlington Industries. **61:** Porterfield-Chickering/Photo Researchers. **64:** NYPL Picture Collection. **66:** Jan Halaska/Photo Researchers. **67:** (T) Louis Goldman/Photo Researchers; (B) William S. Weems/Woodfin Camp. **69:** Bettmann Archive. **71:** Ken Lax/The Image Bank. **76–77:** Dan McCoy/Rainbow. **78:** Townsend/Monkmeyer. **88:** John Eagan. **90:** Kansas City Public Library. **92:** Kansas City Public Library. **97:** Kansas City Public Information Office. **102:** Coco McCoy/Rainbow. **103:** (BL) Denley Carlson/Stock, Boston; (BR) Michal Heron/McGraw-Hill. **104:** Mimi Forsyth/Monkmeyer. **105:** (BL) L. L. T. Rhodes/Taurus; (BR) Carl Byoir. **106:** (BL) Editorial Photocolor Archives; (BR) Michal Heron/McGraw-Hill. **108:** Hallmark. **109:** (TL) Mimi Forsyth/Monkmeyer; (TR) Werner Wolff/Black Star. **110:** Bob Capece/McGraw-Hill. **111:** Mimi Forsyth/Monkmeyer. **113:** (BL) John King/McGraw-Hill; (BR) John King/McGraw-Hill. **115:** Monkmeyer Press Photo. **116:** NYPL Picture Collection. **117:** Russ Kinne/Photo Researchers. **119:** Arthur/Warner Collection/Dallas. **120:** State Capitol, Austin, Texas. **124:** (TL) Thomas Friedman/Photo Researchers; (TR) Craig Aurness/Woodfin Camp. **125:** Owen Franken/Stock, Boston. **127:** George Hall/Woodfin Camp. **132–33:** Craig Aurness/Woodfin Camp. **138:** (TL) Joe Munroe/Photo Researchers; (BL) Bullaty Lomeo/Photo Researchers; (BR) Monkmeyer. **142:** George Hall/Woodfin Camp. **144:** Los Angeles County Museum. **147:** "Cattle Drive," James Walker, California Historical Society. **148:** "Slaughtering of Beef at the Ranch," James Walker, Collection of Mrs. R. Walker. **149:** Title Insurance and Trust Co., Los Angeles. **150:** Culver Pictures. **152:** (TL) Bettmann Archive; (TR) Culver Pictures. **154:** (TH) Harvey Wang; (TR) Leonard Nadal/McGraw-Hill. **155:** Peter Menzel. **156:** (BL), (BR) Leonard Nadal/McGraw-Hill. **158:** Leonard Nadal/McGraw-Hill. **160:** Leonard Nadal/McGraw-Hill. **162:** Hugh Rogers/Monkmeyer. **163:** James Theologos/Monkmeyer. **164:** (BL), (BR) Leonard Nadal/McGraw-Hill. **167:** Chuck O'Rear/Woodfin Camp. **169:** (BL) Brown Brothers; (BR) Honolulu Academy of Arts. **170:** (TL) Paul Conklin/Monkmeyer; (TR) L. L. T. Rhodes/Animals, Animals. **173:** George Hall/Woodfin Camp. **174:** Culver Pictures. **176:** Paul Seaman/Photo Researchers. **177:** Sid Latham/Photo Researchers. **182–183:** Michael Philip Manheim/Photo Researchers. **184:** Earl Roberge/Photo Researchers. **185:** (TL) Canadian Consulate; (TR) Owen Franken/Stock, Boston. **188:** Peter Dublin. **189:** (TR) Peter Dublin; (BL) Toge Fujihara/Stock, Boston; (BR) Kryn Traconis/Stock, Boston. **190:** Stock, Boston. **193:** E. Otto/Miller Services. **194:** Toge Fujihara/Monkmeyer. **195:** Canadian National Film Board. **196:** (TL) Canadian National Film Board; (TR) Miller Services; (BL) Andy Bernhaut/Photo Researchers; (BR) Canadian National Railroad. **198:** Kryn Traconis/Magnum. **200:** Kryn Traconis/Magnum. **202:** McKinney/Miller Services. **204:** Ville De Montreal. **207:** (BL) Peter Dublin; (BR) Owen Franken/Stock, Boston. **208:** Larry Mulvehill/Photo Researchers. **209:** Paolo Koch/Photo Researchers. **211:** (BL) Peter Dublin; (BR) Mia & Klaus, Montreal. **213:** Moshe Safdi & Associates. **214:** Moshe Safdi & Associates. **219:** Victor Englebert/Photo Researchers. **220:** Dick Davis/Photo Researchers. **225:** Michal Heron/McGraw-Hill. **226:** Marc and Evelyne Bernheim/Woodfin Camp. **227:** Porterfield-Chickering/Photo Researchers. **228:** Bendick Associates/Monkmeyer. **230:** NYPL Picture Collection. **231:** H. Bijur/Monkmeyer. **232:** Constantine Manos/Magnum. **234:** NYPL Picture Collection. **235:** American Museum of Natural History. **236:** NYPL Picture Collection. **238:** Helen Marcus/Photo Researchers. **240:** Culver Pictures. **242:** Marc and Evelyne Bernheim/Woodfin Camp. **245:** (BL) Carl Frank/Photo Researchers; (BR) Marc and Evelyne Bernheim/Woodfin Camp. **246:** Marc and Evelyne Bernheim/Woodfin Camp.